RANDOM
HOUSE

LARGE
PRINT

ALSO BY BILL CLINTON
AVAILABLE FROM RANDOM HOUSE LARGE PRINT

Giving

My Life

BILL CLINTON

Back to Work

Why We Need
Smart Government for a
Strong Economy

RANDOM HOUSE
LARGE PRINT

Cover photograph by Andrew Hetherington, 2011
Cover design by Carol Devine Carson

The Library of Congress has established a
Cataloging-in-Publication record for this title.

ISBN: 978-0-307-99073-0

www.randomhouse.com/largeprint

FIRST LARGE PRINT EDITION

Printed in the United States of America

10 9 8 7 6 5 4 3 2 1

This Large Print edition published in accord with
the standards of the N.A.V.H.

To the millions of good people who are looking for the chance to be part of America's recovery, and their own.

CONTENTS

INTRODUCTION

I WROTE THIS BOOK BECAUSE I love my country and I'm concerned about our future. As I often said when I first ran for president in 1992, America at its core is an idea—the idea that no matter who you are or where you're from, if you work hard and play by the rules, you'll have the freedom and opportunity to pursue your own dreams and leave your kids a country where they can chase theirs.

That belief has a tenuous hold on the more than fifteen million people who are unemployed or who are working part-time when they need full-time jobs to support themselves and their families. And it must seem downright unreal to the growing number of men and women who've been out of work for more than six months and can't even get interviews for job openings, as if they're somehow to blame for becoming casualties of the worst recession since the Depression.

Work is about more than making a living, as vital as that is. It's fundamental to human dignity, to our sense of self-worth as useful, independent, free people. I earned my first money mowing lawns when I was twelve. At thirteen, I worked in a small grocery store and set up a used-comic-book stand on the side. By the time I finished college, I'd made a little money doing seven other things. By the end of law school, seven more. Over the last four decades, nine more, not counting my foundation and other philanthropic work. Most of my early jobs didn't last long. I didn't like them all. But I learned something in every job—about the work, dealing with people, and giving employers and customers their money's worth.

I came of age believing that no matter what happened, I would always be able to support myself. It became a crucial part of my identity and drove me to spend a good portion of my adult life trying to give other people the chance to do the same thing. It's heartbreaking to see so many people trapped in a web of enforced idleness, deep debt, and gnawing self-doubt. We have to change that. And we can.

In these few pages, I'll try to explain what has happened to our country over the last thirty years, why our political system hasn't done a better job of meeting our challenges, and why government still matters and what it should do. I'll do my best to clarify what our choices are to revive the economy and deal with our long-term debt, and I'll argue that the looming debt is a big problem that can't be solved unless the economy starts growing again. And I don't mean the kind of jobless, statistical growth of the first decade of the twenty-first century, with stagnant wages, rising poverty, crippling household debt, and 90 percent of the income growth going to the top 10 percent. I want American Dream growth—lots of new businesses, well-paying jobs, and American leadership in new industries, like clean energy and biotechnology.

Unless we restore robust economic growth, we'll be stuck in this economy for years, and nothing we do will solve the longer-term debt problem, regardless of how we try to do it.

In short, we've got to get America back in the future business.

PART I

Where We Are

CHAPTER 1

Our Thirty-Year Antigovernment Obsession

I DECIDED TO WRITE THIS BOOK after the 2010 midterm election not because my party took a beating, but because of what the election was about. The bad economy, the high cost of keeping the recession from falling into full-scale depression, the fact that the recovery had not yet begun to improve many lives—all these ensured that anger and anxiety would be at high tide on Election Day, and that's always bad news for the party in power.

What troubled me is that with so many people hurting and so many challenges to be faced, the election season offered few opportunities for a real discussion of what went wrong, what the president and Congress had actually done or failed to do in the previous two years, what the two parties proposed to do in 2011 and 2012, and what the likely consequences would be in the short and long runs. Nor was there much of substance said on the larger issues on which these questions would have an impact: How do we propose to restore and maintain the American Dream at home? How do we ensure America's economic, political, and security leadership in the more competitive, complex, fragmented, and fast-changing world of the twenty-first century?

Instead, the election seemed to occur in a parallel universe of inflated rhetoric and ferocious but often inaccurate attacks that shed more heat than light. The Republicans seemed to be saying that the financial crash and the recession that followed, as well as the failure of the United States to fully recover from it less than eighteen months after the economy bottomed out, were caused by too much government taxing, spending, and regulating, and that all would be well once we cut the cancer of government out of our lives and pocketbooks. They portrayed Democratic congressional incumbents and the president as big-government liberals who had brought America to the edge of destruction and, if given two more years, would push us over into the abyss.

The attack proved to be very effective in the election, but I thought it was all wrong. **First, the meltdown happened because banks were overleveraged,** with too many risky investments, especially in subprime mortgages and the securities and derivatives that were spun out of them, and too little cash to cover the risks. For example, Bear Stearns was leveraged at thirty-five to one when it failed; traditionally, commercial bank lending is leveraged at ten or twelve to one, investment banking a bit more. In other words, **there was not enough government oversight or restraint on excessive leverage.**

Second, the meltdown did not become a full-scale depression because the government acted to save the financial system from collapse. The Federal Reserve made massive investments of about $1.2 trillion to stop the financial collapse, including buying securities and guaranteeing loans. The often-derided Troubled Asset Relief Program (TARP) was originally authorized to spend up to $700 billion and spent a bit over $400 billion. Most of the TARP money has been paid back, with only $104 billion still outstanding. In a July 8, 2011, **Washington Post** article, Allan Sloan and Doris Burke estimated that the final cost of the TARP program would be just $19 billion and cited an analysis in **Fortune** magazine concluding that the Federal Reserve's income on its investments would produce **a net profit for the taxpayers** on the bailout of between $40 billion and $100 billion.

Third, according to most economic studies, the stimulus, along with the rescue and restructuring of the auto industry, **succeeded in keeping unemployment 1.5 to 2 percent lower than it would have been without it.** Of course, the stimulus didn't restore the economy to normal levels. It wasn't designed to. You can't fill a several-trillion-dollar hole in the economy

with $800 billion. The stimulus was designed to
put a floor under the collapse and begin the recovery. More than a third of the money funded a cut
of about $800 per family in withholding taxes for
95 percent of American families, whose incomes
had increased modestly or not at all in the nearly
eight years before the crash. Many people needed
the money for necessities. About 30 percent of the
money was sent to state and local governments to
prevent larger layoffs of teachers, health workers,
police officers, and other state and local employees.
That part of the stimulus must have worked: After
the funding ceased, state and local government pay-
rolls declined by more than half a million people.

Only a third of the stimulus money went into
direct jobs projects, mostly roads, bridges, and other
infrastructure construction; and into incentives,
loans, and grants to increase the manufacturing of
new clean-energy products and more energy-efficient
technologies. For example, between January 2009,
when President Obama was inaugurated, and Election Day 2010, the United States had gained thirty
new battery plants, built or under construction,
increasing America's share of the world market for
the batteries that power hybrid and all-electric vehicles from 2 percent to 20 percent in less than two
years. We'll have the capacity to fill 40 percent of the
market by 2014, if the incentives are maintained.

In other words, the crash occurred because there
was too little government oversight of and virtually

no restraint on risky loans without sufficient capital to back them up; the recession was prevented from becoming a depression because of a government infusion of cash to shore up the banking system; and the downturn hurt fewer people because of the stimulus, which supplemented wages with a tax cut, saved public jobs, and created jobs through infrastructure projects and incentives to create private-sector jobs, especially in manufacturing.

The success of the Republicans' antigovernment attack was doubly surprising to me, because of their own record over the previous eight years. They cut taxes and increased spending at roughly twice the rate it had increased during my eight years in office, creating few new jobs but ending four years of balanced budgets and surpluses and **doubling the national debt even before the financial meltdown.** And, of course, they also regularly voted to raise the debt limit so they could continue to borrow and spend, a practice I had worked hard to end.

When the Democrats regained a majority in Congress in 2007, they inherited an already severe mortgage crisis and very weak job growth. By the time President Obama was inaugurated, we had been in a recession for more than a year, and the financial crash in September 2008 had turned it into the worst downturn since the Depression, sending both the annual deficit and the total national debt even higher. Something had to be done to stop the decline. Immediately, the antigovernment movement reversed course. After eight years in which the Republicans had increased spending at a rapid rate, they opposed spending by the new president and Congress to put a floor under the recession, and they began blaming the Democrats for the explosion of debt caused by their own policies and the crash.

ONE OF THE MOST INTERESTING THINGS to me is how easy it was to persuade so many Americans, even those who rely on government programs, to join in the government-bashing. One congressman was captured on camera looking dumbfounded at a town hall meeting on health-care reform when an angry constituent shouted that he didn't want the government "messing with my Medicare"! In Arkansas, which has a large agricultural economy, farmers who had always lobbied hard for agricultural supports voted against the first Arkansan ever to chair the Senate Agriculture Committee, Senator Blanche Lincoln, because she was for "too much government." As far as I could tell, her main contributions to "big government" were sponsoring a big increase in nutrition aid for poor children, which also helped farmers; passing an amendment to the financial reform bill that requires the derivatives sold by traders on Wall Street to be as transparent and financially sound as the agricultural derivatives farmers buy to hedge against losses from yields or prices that are too low; and saving more than a thousand factory jobs by insisting that the federal government enforce the rules against unfair trade practices. And she voted for the health-care bill, which postelection analysis showed cost Democrats in Republican-leaning areas about 6 percent of the vote. I think it was the right vote, especially for a state like Arkansas, with lots of uninsured small businesses and working families who will now be able to afford health insurance. But on Election Day, it looked like too much government.

Now, in 2011, Republicans and Democrats in Congress and in the White House are locked in a pitched battle over how and how much to cut our annual deficit at a time when our economic recovery remains shaky. Republicans say they will tolerate no new taxes, even on upper-income individuals who reaped almost all the income gains of the last decade (90 percent to the top 10 percent; more than 60 percent to the top 1 percent and more than 20 percent to people with incomes over $9 million), with multiple tax cuts, to boot. They opposed the stimulus in part because the tax cuts only went to the bottom 95 percent. For months, they threatened to refuse to raise the debt limit, which allows the government to borrow money to pay bills it has already incurred, a move that would further harm the recovery. If we ever refused to honor our obligations, the government's credit rating would be downgraded. Americans would pay higher interest rates across the board, on credit card purchases and on small-business, home mortgage, car, and college loans. The government's annual interest payments on our national debt would also rise, further increasing the deficit.

For reasons that are unclear, the president and the Democratic Congress did not raise the debt ceiling after the election, in November or December 2010, when they still had a majority. Given that fact, as well as the president's duty to go the extra mile to avoid a default, the last-minute agreement in early August 2011 between the House Speaker, both Senate leaders, and the White House to raise the debt limit in return for $2.5 trillion in budget cuts over a decade and no new revenues could have been a lot worse. It requires $1 trillion in spending cuts over the next decade, followed by an agreement early in 2012 to cut $1.5 trillion more, after Congress gets recommendations from a twelve-member committee of its members, made up of six senators and six representatives, equally divided by party. Democrats won the concession that Medicare, Medicaid, Social Security, and a planned increase in Pell Grants* would be exempt from the first round of cuts, a mixed blessing. And in the first year, 2012, only $21 billion of the $1 trillion will be cut, a concession to the weakness of the economy.

*Unlike student loans, Pell Grants don't have to be repaid. The maximum grant is $5,550 for the 2011–12 academic year, with a student's actual amount determined by financial need, the cost of attending a particular school, and whether the student is full-time or part-time.

The whole debt ceiling/deficit reduction debate process was an extreme example of why Mark Twain said the only two things people should never watch being made are sausage and laws. To the outside world, the United States looked weak and confused, completely in the grip of the antigovernment zealots in the House Republican caucus, with Democrats unable to use their Senate majority to pass a bigger, more balanced plan of cuts and taxes, because they hadn't raised the debt ceiling when they had the chance and the antigovernment ideologues were willing to default on our debt to get their way. Representative Michele Bachmann, a Tea Party favorite, even endorsed a default, describing it as a needed dose of "tough love."

SHORTLY AFTER THE AGREEMENT WAS ANNOUNCED, one rating agency, Standard & Poor's (S&P), downgraded America's long-term credit rating anyway. The decision was criticized in many quarters because no one doubted the ability of the United States to pay its debts. The nation has total assets valued at just under $60 trillion. Progressive commentators blasted the decision as hypocritical, because S&P, along with other rating agencies, consistently gave high ratings to the subprime mortgage securities that were far riskier than U.S. Treasury bonds. Some wondered whether S&P's double standard was rooted in the fact that the rating agencies are financed by pay-

ments from the securities industry. Others said that
S&P erred in concluding that the debt deal was too
small to "stabilize the government's medium-term
debt dynamics" because the agency overstated the
size of the debt by $2 trillion.

S&P stated clearly that what really upset it was
the politics of Washington, the slow recovery from
the recession, and the fact that over the next few
years debt in several wealthy countries is projected
to go down as a percentage of GDP but the U.S.
debt probably will not do so, mostly because the
United States, alone among wealthy nations, has had
no effective restraint on health-care costs. Above all,
S&P thinks America's politics have become dysfunc-
tional. Their assessment sounds like Mark Twain's
comparison of lawmaking to sausage-making—on
steroids, and without the humor.

I HAVE STARTED AND STOPPED this project several
times over the last few months because politics is
no longer the center of my working life and I don't
want just to add another stone to the Democratic
side of the partisan scale.

I decided to go forward because I think it's important that all Americans have a clear understanding
of the basic economic facts and of the ideas driving
the policy proposals under discussion. For example,
even though I strongly favor a multiyear plan to
bring our budget back into balance, if we cut spend-

ing or raise taxes a lot when the economy is still weak, it will slow down economic recovery. Unlike the situation in 1993, when my deficit reduction plan sparked a substantial drop in interest rates and a big increase in private investment, interest rates today are already near zero. So in the short run, a big cut in spending could even increase the annual deficit, because tax revenues might decrease even more than government spending is cut. The problem today is weak demand for new goods, services, and labor, reinforced by the huge drag of the unresolved home mortgage crisis.

I believe the challenges we face, which are tough enough on their own, are made even more difficult by the highly polarized, deeply ideological political climate in Washington. It is an almost alien environment to me now, because the what I do today—in my foundation, in the Clinton Global Initiative, and in Haiti—is a world away from Washington's political wars. We receive support from Democrats, Republicans, independents, and concerned citizens the world over. Instead of focusing on our differences, we come together to build a world of shared opportunities and shared responsibilities. Instead of making speeches, we focus on taking action on our common challenges, and on keeping score, so that we learn what works and what doesn't. Whenever possible, we collaborate with both government and the private sector to do things better, faster, and at lower costs.

It seems to be working: helping more than four million people with AIDS in developing countries get lifesaving medicine; increasing farmers' incomes in Latin America and Africa; developing pro-growth approaches to fighting climate change around the world; fighting childhood obesity in the United States by reducing calories in drinks consumed by kids in schools by 88 percent; offering America's first master's degree in public service, as opposed to public policy, at the University of Arkansas's Clinton School of Public Service; and building global networks of givers whose commitments at the Clinton Global Initiative have already helped more than 300 million people in 170 countries.

I've been honored to work with both President George H. W. Bush on rebuilding efforts after the tsunami in south Asia and Hurricane Katrina and with President George W. Bush in Haiti to rebuild and diversify the economy there in the aftermath of the earthquake. After the tsunami I worked for two years as the UN secretary-general's representative to the affected countries, as I have done in Haiti since 2008. Now I also work with the prime minister of Haiti, and with representatives of Haitian society and donor nations, to approve major projects and to assure their transparency and accountability.

Doing this work in America and around the world, after eight years as president and twelve years as governor of Arkansas, has given me a lot of exposure to how the twenty-first-century world functions, the challenges America faces in making the most of it, and the barriers to meeting these challenges that the current debate in Washington has created.

We live in the most interdependent age in history. People are increasingly likely to be affected by actions beyond their borders, and their borders are increasingly open to both positive and negative crossings: travelers, immigrants, money, goods, services, information, communication, and culture; disease, trafficking in drugs, weapons, and people, and acts of terrorism and violent crime.

The modern world has many attractions—scientific advances, technological breakthroughs, instant information-sharing, greater social diversity, and the empowerment of people everywhere through cell phones and the Internet. But as we all know, people everywhere also face severe challenges, most of which can be grouped into three categories. The modern world is **too unequal** in incomes and in access to jobs, health, and education. It is **too unstable**, as evidenced by the rapid spreading of the financial crisis, economic insecurity, political upheavals, and our shared vulnerability to terrorism. And the world's growth pattern is **unsustainable**, because the way we produce and use energy and deplete natural resources is causing climate change and other environmental problems.

No matter what the naysayers claim, the evidence is overwhelming that the climate is changing because of human activity, and if we don't change course quickly and sharply, the consequences are going to be terrible. The signs are all around us, in rising temperatures (nine of the hottest ten years on record occurred in the last thirteen years), melting ice caps, rising sea levels, more droughts, fires, floods, and severe storms. My native state of Arkansas is in America's tornado alley just south of Joplin, Missouri, which was recently devastated by an especially powerful tornado. But in 2010 and 2011, tornadoes also hit in Queens in New York City and in Massachusetts, areas in the Northeast where they're all but unheard of.

Though these problems are affecting the lives of people in every nation, responding to them effectively presents very different challenges to poor and rich nations. Poor nations have to build systems that those of us in wealthy nations take for granted— economic, financial, education, health-care, energy, environmental, government service, and other systems that make prosperity and security possible and provide predictable rewards to citizens for hard work and honest dealing. Haiti is now trying to build such systems. When poor countries succeed in doing that, their citizens are able to rapidly increase their incomes, as Vietnam, Rwanda, and other developing nations have proven over the last fifteen years.

Wealthy countries have such systems; they were built on the road to prosperity. The challenge is to keep them working, and improving, as times and conditions change, because at some point the people who run them and those who benefit from them inevitably become resistant to change: more committed to holding on to their positions than to advancing the purposes for which they were established in the first place; more interested in holding on to or increasing present advantages than in creating greater opportunities for others and a brighter future for our children. You can see these forces at work in the politics of Washington: The status quo is represented by much more powerful lobbying groups than the future is.

Because the world is still organized around nations, the decisions national leaders make and citizens support today determine tomorrow's possibilities. For poor countries, that means building systems that give more and more people a chance to have decent jobs and send their kids to school. For rich countries, it means reforming systems that once worked well but no longer do, so people can keep moving forward in an increasingly complex and competitive environment.

That's what America has to do. **We have to get back in the future business.** And that's why politics, with all its frustrations and distractions, is still important. Over the last three decades, whenever we've given in to the temptation to blame the government for all our problems, we've lost our commitment to shared prosperity, balanced growth, financial responsibility, and investment in the future. That's really what got us into trouble.

Even before the financial crash, the economy had produced only 2.5 million jobs in the previous seven years and eight months; median family income after inflation was $2,000 lower than it was the day I left office; income inequality and poverty had increased; and home mortgage foreclosures were exploding. Almost all our economic growth was fueled by home building, consumer spending, and finance, all based on easy credit and heavy leverage. We lost manufacturing jobs every year. Ordinary citizens maxed out their credit cards to keep consumption up as they struggled with flat incomes and rising costs, especially for health care, which increased at three times the rate of inflation.

As the government abandoned balanced budgets in 2001 for big tax cuts and large spending increases, the national debt, which had decreased from 49 percent to 33 percent of national income in the 1990s, soared back to 62 percent in 2010. Consumer debt went from 84 percent of average income in the 1990s to a high of 127 percent in 2007. Since the crash, savings have increased a bit, and some debts have been written off, but our citizens' debt is still at 112 percent of average income.

This is not the way I wanted the United States to start the twenty-first century. I did my best as president to prepare America for it—to create jobs, raise incomes, and reduce poverty; to improve the quality of our air, food, and water and preserve irreplaceable natural treasures; to increase our competitiveness in the global economy by maintaining our leadership in science, technology, innovation, and access to higher education; to alert the nation to the dangers of climate change and the economic benefits of avoiding them; and to increase our security by promoting peace and prosperity around the world while increasing our ability to deter and prevent security threats, especially from terrorists and the proliferation of and trafficking in nuclear, chemical, and biological weapons.

We pursued that agenda while keeping taxes under 20 percent of GDP and spending under 19 percent. When I left office, the United States was in position to become debt-free within twelve to fifteen years, handle the retirement of the baby boomers, and make the investments required to keep the American Dream alive in the twenty-first century.

I didn't succeed in every endeavor, and I made some mistakes in trying. But overall, the United States was better off at the dawn of the twenty-first century than we had been eight years earlier. I think one reason is that we began by asking the right questions: How can we build a nation and a world of shared benefits and shared responsibilities? How can we accelerate the spread of the positive and reduce the reach of the negative forces that affect us all? What is the proper role of government? What should America expect from and promote in the private sector? What about civil society, the nongovernmental organizations that have been important to us since our founding? How can we appreciate, cultivate, and profit from our diversity while reaffirming that our common humanity and shared values matter more?

During the campaign of 2010 and for most of the last thirty years, our political debates have not been about answering those questions. Instead, beginning with President Reagan's campaign in 1980, we have been told that all America's problems are caused by government, by taxes that are too high, bureaucracies that are too big, regulations that are too costly and intrusive—if we just had less of all that, free people would solve all their problems on their own.

Americans have always had heated debates about what government should and shouldn't do. Because we were founded in reaction to the unaccountable and overreaching power of British colonialism, we've often been of two minds: we don't want too much government, but we want enough. How much is enough but not too much is the traditional dividing line between liberals and conservatives. The debate changed in 1980. As President Reagan declared in his first inaugural address, "Government is the problem." If government is the problem, the question is always, "How can we get less of it?" If you ask the right questions, you may not always get the right answers. But if you ask the wrong questions, you can't get the right answers.

I believe the only way we can keep the American Dream alive for all Americans and continue to be the world's leading force for freedom and prosperity, peace and security, is to have **both** a strong, effective private sector **and** a strong, effective government that work together to promote an economy of good jobs, rising incomes, increasing exports, and greater energy independence. All over the world, the most successful nations, including many with lower unemployment rates, less inequality, and, in this decade, even higher college graduation rates than the United States, have **both**. And they work together, not always agreeing, but moving toward common goals. In other countries, conservatives and liberals also have arguments about taxes, energy policy, bank regulations, and how much government is healthy and affordable, but they tend to be less ideological and more rooted in evidence and experience. **They focus more on what works.**

That's the focus America needs. It's the only way to get back into the future business. In the modern world, when too few citizens have the time or opportunity to analyze the larger forces shaping our lives, and the lines between news, advocacy, and entertainment are increasingly blurred, ideological conflicts effectively waged may be good politics, and provide fodder for the nightly news, talk shows, and columnists, but they won't get us to a better future.

Our long antigovernment obsession has proved to be remarkably successful politics, but its policy failures have given us an anemic, increasingly unequal economy, with too few jobs and stagnant incomes;

put us at a competitive disadvantage compared with other nations, especially in manufacturing and clean energy; and left us a potentially crippling debt burden just as the baby boomers begin to retire.

By contrast, other nations, as well as states and cities within the United States, with a commitment to building networks of cooperation involving the public, private, and nonprofit sectors, are creating economic opportunity and charging into the future with confidence.

My argument here isn't that Democrats are always right and Republicans always wrong. It's that by jamming all issues into the antigovernment, antitax, antiregulation straitjacket, we hog-tie ourselves and keep ourselves from making necessary changes no matter how much evidence exists to support them. The antigovernment paradigm blinds us to possibilities that lie outside its ideological litmus tests and prevents us from creating new networks of cooperation that can restore economic growth, bring economic opportunity to more people and places, and increase our ability to lead the world to a better future.

To develop an effective strategy to get the jobs engine going again and deal with our long-term debt problem, we have to take off the blinders of antigovernment ideology and focus on what role government must play in America's renewal.

CHAPTER 2

The 2010 Election
and Its Place in the History
of Antigovernment Politics

IN THE 2010 ELECTION CYCLE, I agreed to do
a number of events, both fund-raisers and ral-
lies, for people who had supported Hillary in the
2008 presidential primaries, because as secretary of
state she can't participate in partisan politics and I
wanted to honor their support for her. Somewhere
along the way I began trying to help other Democrats too, in what grew to more than 130 events,
because I believed President Obama and Congress
had done a better job than they were getting credit
for and because the Republican proposals to repeal
health-care reform, college-loan reform, financial-
regulation reform, and clean-energy investments;
cancel the unspent stimulus funding; and enact

more large tax cuts and big spending cuts across the board represented an even more extreme version of the thirty-year-old antigovernment philosophy that got us into trouble in the first place.

I tried to explain in plain language what the president and Congress had accomplished in the previous two years and what both parties were proposing to do in the next two. I explained why I thought the Democrats offered America a better chance to revive the economy and create jobs, increase health coverage and quality and slow the rise in health-care costs, prevent future financial meltdowns and more bailouts, reverse the alarming decline in college-graduation rates, and, as the economy recovers, bring our budget back into balance.

I also tried to get a few laughs to break the tension that hard times bring by joking that my feelings were hurt because I wasn't the Tea Party's favorite political figure. After all, during my administration we had four surplus budgets and began to pay down the national debt; we eliminated sixteen thousand pages of federal regulations; we cut taxes on the middle class, working families of modest means, and income from capital gains; we reduced welfare rolls by almost 60 percent; we reduced the size of the federal workforce to its lowest level since 1960, when Dwight Eisenhower was president, and the smallest percentage of the overall workforce since 1933; and the economy produced more jobs (92 percent in the private sector, the largest percentage in fifty years) and moved a hundred times more people out of poverty than in the Reagan years (7.7 million versus 77,000).

I couldn't win the Tea Party over, of course, because the actions they agreed with weren't the whole story. We balanced the budget with a balanced plan: with both spending cuts and tax increases on the wealthiest corporations and individuals (the top 1.2 percent) who had benefited disproportionately from America's growth and from tax cuts in the 1980s; strengthened regulations to get cleaner air and water and safer food; appointed an SEC commissioner who believed in firm oversight of investment banking practices; set aside more land for preservation in the lower forty-eight states than any president since Teddy Roosevelt; added years to Medicare's and Social Security's solvency; doubled spending on education, including the largest increase in aid to college students since the GI Bill; spent more on education, transportation, and child care to help people move from welfare to work; achieved almost universal access to the Internet in schools, hospitals, and libraries; doubled investment in biomedical research and created the Children's Health Insurance Program, the biggest expansion of health coverage since Medicare and Medicaid; created the COPS program, which put 100,000 police on America's streets; and enacted the Brady Bill and the assault weapons ban, leading to the longest continuous drop in crime in our history—all ideological nonstarters for passionate antigovernment advocates, but all good for America.

Of course, speeches by a former president don't sway many votes, especially in the face of a disciplined, intense, well-financed campaign, but I tried. The big defeat didn't surprise me, but it did leave me deeply concerned for the future of our country, because of the leading role played by antigovernment activists, who were sure to interpret the results as an endorsement of their most extreme proposals.

There were many reasons for the magnitude of the defeat. First, the size of the Democratic majority before 2011 was in large part a reaction to the years of one-party GOP rule, years in which the economy produced very few jobs, mortgage foreclosures exploded, and opposition to the war in Iraq intensified. In 2006, Democrats won back majorities in both houses of Congress for the first time since 1994. Then the financial meltdown in September 2008 in effect decided the presidential election and ensured that even more Democrats would go to Congress. Many of those elected in 2006 and 2008 represented districts that were not normally Democratic.

Second, the people had given both the White House and Congress to Democrats to fix things, and on Election Day 2010 things didn't feel fixed. Jobs weren't coming back, and the deficit continued to increase dramatically, due to the combination of declining revenues because of lower incomes and higher unemployment and increased federal spending, because of the stimulus package and the large number of unemployed people and part-time workers who were receiving aid. For example, one in seven Americans was getting food stamps. So even though President Obama and Congress did several significant, positive things in 2009 and 2010, the beneficiaries of the changes didn't yet feel them, and often didn't even know about them, while the opponents of those changes were inflamed and energized.

Third, Americans hate all the partisan bickering in Washington and usually prefer to see one party in control of Congress when the other is in the White House. They think that will force our elected officials to work together across party lines and keep the government from going too far to the left or the right. So in 2010, whether it was necessary or not, the whirlwind of government activity—saving the financial system, the stimulus, restructuring the auto industry, the financial reforms, the health-care law—left many voters thinking we had too much government. That's what happened in 1994, too, when independent voters also rewarded the partisan "just say no" tactics they otherwise deplore.

Fourth, the Republicans ran a more effective, more aggressive campaign, characterizing the Speaker of the House, Nancy Pelosi, the Senate majority leader, Harry Reid, and President Obama as extreme leftists who wanted to spend America into ruin, regulate the economy into extended recession, and tax individuals into poverty and businesses into bank-ruptcy: Someone had to stop them before it was too late. The GOP candidates repeated the message incessantly, as did their supporters in the media and interest groups.

The Republicans were also both candid and clever in presenting their own policy agenda in printed materials distributed to their more ideological base voters. They proposed (1) to cancel the still-unspent portion of the "failed" stimulus, in spite of nonpar-tisan studies finding that the stimulus had created more jobs than predicted and kept unemployment lower than it would have been; (2) to repeal the financial-reform bill with its provisions to require banks to maintain more capital to cover potential loan losses and to avoid future bailouts by establish-ing a liquidation procedure that would hold stock-holders and management more accountable for them (so repeal would make both failures and the bailouts the Tea Party claims to deplore more likely in the future); (3) to repeal incentives to rebuild our manufacturing base through green technologies and instead rely on more drilling for oil and gas, min-ing coal, and spending on heavily subsidized nuclear power;* (4) to repeal the student-loan reform law, ending direct government lending, giving a 90 per-

---

*In the 2005 Energy Policy Act, Congress agreed in effect to insure the nuclear industry against losses in building new power plants, since no private insurance company will issue policies to do so.

cent government guarantee to banks to make loans, rendering them more expensive, thus increasing the costs to taxpayers and eliminating the most important part of the law—the part that allows students to repay their debt as a small percentage of their income for up to twenty years, so they won't ever have to drop out again for fear they'll never be able to repay their debt;* (5) to repeal the health-care reform law, including the requirement that insurance companies spend 85 percent of the premiums people pay on health-care costs (80 percent for smaller plans), not on profits or marketing; to reverse the so-called cuts in Medicare, which were actually lower increases in reimbursement rates to providers, especially in the Medicare Advantage program, where the profit margins of the participating private providers were large; and, having given the money back to the providers, to reopen the so-called doughnut hole in the senior citizens' drug program and reduce the solvency of Medicare by a few years;† and (6) to both cut taxes again, largely for upper-income citizens, and still reduce the large annual deficit by making very large

*The student loan reform law will actually cost $60 billion less over ten years than the current system. The bill allocated $40 billion to increasing Pell Grants and other student aid, with the remaining $20 billion applied against the debt. So repeal actually increases the debt!

†The cuts apparently had no adverse impact on Medicare Advantage. In 2011, a record number of private companies applied to the Department of Health and Human Services to provide the program's services to seniors.

but unspecified cuts in nondefense, non-Medicare spending.

The fifth reason for the size of the Republican victory is that for the first time since their big losses in 1994, when the Republicans ran on the Contract with America, the Democrats did not counter the national Republican message with one of their own. There was no national advertising campaign to explain and defend what they had done and to compare their agenda for the next two years with the GOP proposals. The large amount of money Democrats raised, $1.6 billion, was almost all spent on local races, just as it was in 1994, with similar results.

In the 1998, 2002, and 2006 midterm elections, the Democrats did well with a national message buttressed by a few clear specifics, winning House seats in 1998 despite being badly outspent, the first time since 1822 the president's party had won House seats in the sixth year of a presidency; not losing many seats in 2002, with President Bush and national security riding high in the polls in the aftermath of 9/11; and in 2006, with the economy in bad shape and the Iraq War increasingly unpopular, winning the majority in both houses of Congress for the first time since 1994.

In 2010, with the economy in trouble, people upset with government spending that didn't seem to be making it better, and many Democrats holding seats in Republican-leaning districts facing energized, organized opposition, the Democrats ran individual races without a big message. Apparently, they couldn't agree on one, because they themselves were divided on some issues, especially health care and how best to combat climate change. These problems could have been finessed with commitments to reform—not repeal—the health-care law and to change how we produce and consume energy in a way that grows the economy and creates jobs.

Vice President Biden—whose speeches provided much of the same information and made many of the same arguments mine did—and I tried to get the Democratic National Committee to send out a centralized set of talking points to its large e-mail list so Democratic foot soldiers would at least have some good ammunition for their phone and door-to-door campaigns. We couldn't persuade the decision makers to do so. I'm always glad to be in Joe Biden's company, but it was frustrating to work crowds, right up to the night before the election, and hear people shouting at us after our speeches, "Why didn't I know that?" At least we know Democrats can keep a secret. The failure to counter the GOP national campaign with an equally good one cost the Democrats.

Beyond the economic turmoil, the popular inclination toward divided government, and the relative effectiveness of the campaigns, there is a final factor that had a large impact on the election and the partisan wrangling on the budget that followed it: the

idea that the government, especially the federal government, is the cause of every problem America has.
Therefore, no matter what the problem, apart from
national security, the solution is always the same:
less government, lower taxes, weaker regulations.

At its core, this has been the modern Republican
Party's credo since President Reagan rode it to victory in 1980. The idea that the government would
mess up a two-car parade has shaped the framework
in which we debate the issues and colored the way
the media reports on them. It's great politics for antigovernment Republicans because it meets the financial needs of their biggest backers and the emotional
needs of alienated voters and, until things get really
bad, explains even the failures of their own admin-
istrations. If you don't believe in government, how
can you be disappointed when it fails? It's supposed
to fail.

The antigovernment theme has also proved to
be irresistible as a framework for members of the
mainstream media, who use the term "conservative"
to describe even the most extreme antigovernment
policies and define as "liberals" all those who oppose
them. This simple but superficial labeling reinforces
an easy but inaccurate caricature of our traditional
political philosophies and makes it harder to understand the likely consequences of radical actions cam-
ouflaged in conservative clothing.

There are only two forces that seem to slow down
extreme antigovernment activists. One is stinging

public rejection, as we saw in the 2011 special election in New York, where a Democrat, Kathy Hochul, won in an overwhelmingly Republican district less than a year after the GOP's landslide victory there by opposing the Ryan plan, which the House had voted for, to replace Medicare with vouchers and require seniors to pay much more out of pocket for health care. The other is progress under a Democratic administration, as was the case in 2000, when George W. Bush ran as a "compassionate conservative" in a time of shared prosperity and more confidence in government.

Then-governor Bush was genuine in his commitment to diversity in government, to improved learning in public schools, to immigration reform, and to doing more to help poor nations fight AIDS. But his brilliant "compassionate conservative" slogan also embodied a more subtle version of the antigovernment theme. Like the Republicans in 2010, Bush was both forthright in making specific antitax, antiregulation commitments targeted to his base and skilled in not pushing them too hard on swing voters who might have disagreed but were captivated by the appeal of his more moderate compassionate-conservative mantra. He was really telling swing voters he'd get them the same good economic results of the previous eight years with a smaller government and lower taxes. Who could be against that?

To be fair, antigovernment politics have been

around a long time, and a healthy skepticism of government power and enforceable limits on its abuse are important to the functioning of any democracy. Criticizing the government is part of the birthright of every American. We can all come up with a program we thought was a waste of money, a regulation we thought was wrong, a tax we thought was too high, and an official we thought went overboard in the exercise of authority.

Our nation was founded by citizens determined to resist—then break away from—an empire ruled by a government unaccountable to them. Our constitution, with its separation of powers and Bill of Rights, is designed to preserve liberty and protect us from abuse of government power. However, contrary to the current antigovernment movement's claim to represent the intent of the framers, our founding fathers clearly intended to give us a **government both limited and accountable enough to protect our liberties and strong and flexible enough to adapt to the challenges of each new era.** They tried to give us the ability to keep America moving toward a "more perfect Union," the eternal mission to which they pledged their lives, fortunes, and sacred honor.

In other words, our constitution was designed by people who were idealistic but not ideological. There's a big difference. You can have a philosophy that tends to be liberal or conservative but still be open to evidence, experience, and argument. That enables people with honest differences to find practical, principled compromise. On the other hand, fervent insistence on an ideology makes evidence, experience, and argument irrelevant: If you possess the absolute truth, those who disagree are by definition wrong, and evidence of success or failure is irrelevant. There is nothing to learn from the experience of other countries. Respectful arguments are a waste of time. Compromise is weakness. And if your policies fail, you don't abandon them; instead, you double down, asserting that they would have worked if only they had been carried to their logical extreme.

A congressional hearing on climate change in March 2011 offered an interesting example of the difference between conservative philosophy and antigovernment ideology. Congressman Ralph Hall, chairman of the House Science, Space, and Technology Committee, convened a hearing to secure testimony from Dr. Richard Muller, a professor of physics at the University of California at Berkeley, who had long been considered a "climate skeptic." Muller started the Berkeley Earth Surface Temperature project with a team of UC physicists and statisticians to conduct an independent review of the research data in order to challenge the overwhelming scientific consensus that global warming is real, is caused primarily by human behavior, and is likely to have calamitous consequences. The project's biggest private backer is the Charles G. Koch Charitable

Foundation, established by one of the Koch brothers, conservative oil billionaires who have also funded efforts to defeat proposals to reduce the burning of fossil fuels for transportation and electricity, two of the largest sources of the greenhouse gases that cause climate change.

The committee members who don't believe climate change is happening or, if it is, don't think it's a problem expected Dr. Muller to support them in their drive to stop the Environmental Protection Agency (EPA) from regulating greenhouse gases by casting doubt on the climate science. Instead, Muller, a supposedly reliable ally, committed an unforgivable error: He was more interested in finding the truth than in confirming the ideological convictions of his supporters. In forthright language, he explained that his project had assembled 1.6 billion temperature measurements and attempted to correct for potential biases he thought might have influenced previous studies. Then he said that as a result of his own review, "We see a global warming trend that is very similar to that previously reported by other groups."

The **Los Angeles Times** reported that "conservative critics who had expected Muller's group to demonstrate a bias among climate scientists reacted with disappointment." Disappointment is putting it mildly. Muller's testimony was ideological heresy, a rejection of the predetermined truth that global warming is a hoax. But Ken Caldeira, a climate scientist at the Carnegie Institution for Science, which also contributed funds to the Berkeley project, praised Muller's statement for acknowledging that previous climate studies "basically got it right. . . . Willingness to revise views in the face of empirical data is the hallmark of the good scientific process."*

It's also the hallmark of good public policy. When our economic plan passed in 1993, it was a comprehensive program of spending cuts, targeted increases in spending on education, technology, and research, tax cuts to spur investment in areas of high unemployment and to help lower-income working families, and tax increases on the largest corporations and the top 1.2 percent of Americans who had reaped most of the income gains and tax cuts of the 1980s. All the Republicans voted against it, claiming the tax increases would crush the economy, calling them a "job killer" and "a one-way ticket to recession."† They were wrong, off the mark by 22.7 million jobs. But today, with federal taxes at their lowest share of national income in fifty years, they're still saying the same thing.

That's really why no comprehensive long-term agreement came out of the 2011 budget negotiations. The central tenet of antigovernment ideol-

*Margot Roosevelt, "Critics' Review Unexpectedly Supports Scientific Consensus on Global Warming," **Los Angeles Times**, April 4, 2011.

†Bill Clinton, **My Life** (New York: Knopf, 2004), p. 537.

ogy is that all tax hikes, even when coupled with much larger spending cuts, are bad. The evidence is irrelevant.

It hasn't always been that way. Previous Republican presidents did not hesitate to invest tax money and use the power of government when the evidence supported doing so. Abraham Lincoln, a self-made man who said society needs wealthy people to encourage industry and enterprise in others, got Congress to fund the transcontinental railroad and, in the heat of the Civil War, signed the Morrill Act, which set aside land in each state on which to establish public universities. Theodore Roosevelt used the power of the federal government to manage our transition from an agricultural to an industrial society, limiting monopolies' power to fix prices and to abuse women and children in the workplace and protecting vast tracts of western lands from private development. Dwight Eisenhower built the Interstate Highway System with tax dollars and sent federal troops to Little Rock, Arkansas, to enforce the Supreme Court's decision on school integration. Richard Nixon signed legislation establishing the Occupational Safety and Health Administration and the EPA, signed an executive order strengthening the federal affirmative action program, and for the first time since World War II imposed wage and price controls to fend off inflation.

Even after the dawn of the antigovernment era, President Reagan signed budgets that restored a sizable portion of the revenues lost to his big tax cuts, including a bill that stabilized the Social Security system for twenty-five years by adjusting benefits and raising taxes. President George H. W. Bush signed the Americans with Disabilities Act; strong amendments to the Clean Air Act to limit smog, acid rain, and emissions of toxic chemicals; and the budget reforms of 1991, which restrained spending, established the PAYGO rule, and modestly raised taxes.* And President George W. Bush supported the No Child Left Behind law; the senior citizens drug benefit; President's Emergency Plan for AIDS Relief (PEPFAR), which provided unprecedented American support for the global fight against AIDS and malaria; and large investments in nation-building in Iraq and Afghanistan.

In fact, the first three decades of the antigovernment movement have been more antitax and anti-regulation than antispending. The lone exception, before 2011, is the yearlong budget battle I waged with the pre–Tea Party antigovernment Congress in 1995 over their plan to dramatically cut education, health, and environmental spending. In a failed effort to force those of us who disagreed with them to give in to their demands, they shut the gov-

---

*I was one of two governors representing the states in working with the Reagan White House on welfare reform in 1987–88 and with the Bush White House on developing national education goals in 1990. Both efforts were serious, cooperative attempts to solve problems in a way that involved Congress and the states, without regard to party.

ernment down, twice. After public opinion moved clearly toward my position, we finally got down to the people's business, agreeing on a reasonable budget, then the Balanced Budget Act, which produced the first of four surplus budgets in a row for the first time in seventy years.

President Obama faces a different challenge. Because of the deep recession, he didn't repeal the Bush tax cuts when the Democrats were in the majority in 2009 and 2010. Instead, to shore up a suffering economy, he enacted both more tax cuts and more spending. Now he's trying to convince Republicans to agree to a long-term deficit-reduction plan that includes both spending cuts and new tax revenues. I didn't have to do that. Even in 1993 with a Democratic Congress, the budget with its spending cuts and tax increases passed by just one vote in the House and one in the Senate, with Vice President Gore breaking a tie.

President Reagan's budget director David Stockman has explained how the era of large permanent deficits began in 1981. At first, the Reagan administration thought that by cutting taxes, they could force big cuts in domestic spending. But when it turned out that the White House and both parties in Congress wanted to keep on spending, they simply borrowed the money to do it. It was the first time in our history that we had deliberately amassed large deficits in peacetime. Unlike President Obama's two-year stimulus program, the 1980s deficit spending was, in effect, a government stimulus program that continued for more than a decade.

At first, because we had a relatively small debt that was mostly held by Americans, the deficit spending led to significant job growth. It was like eating all the candy you want and never having to go to the dentist, though even then the income gains it produced were disproportionately concentrated in the top 10 percent of earners. By 1990, there was enough concern about the rapidly increasing debt that the Democratic Congress passed, and President Bush signed, a budget that began to do something about it. The most highly publicized features of the 1990 budget were a few modest tax increases and the so-called PAYGO rule, which required Congress to fund new programs either by cutting other spending or by raising revenue.

At the time, several moderate Republican representatives, including Minority Leader Bob Michel of Illinois, supported the bill. It was the right thing to do, a responsible first step. However, the antigovernment bloc in the House, led by Newt Gingrich, opposed the budget, using inflammatory language to characterize Republicans who voted for it and the president who signed it as traitors to the antitax cause and, in President Bush's case, as breaking the famous "Read my lips: no new taxes" pledge he made in his 1988 speech to the Republican National Convention.

Though the budget passed, the fight over it was

a political victory for the antigovernment forces. Among House Republicans, Bob Michel emerged weaker, Minority Whip Newt Gingrich stronger. And President Bush's prospects for reelection lessened when he drew a vigorous primary challenge from Pat Buchanan, who harped on the broken "no new taxes" promise.

Though I was the ultimate beneficiary of the president's misfortune, I couldn't help feeling sympathy for his dilemma. He got the worst of both worlds. First, job creation virtually ground to a halt during his term, the inevitable consequence of what he had rightly called "voodoo economics" during his first run for president in 1980. By the late 1980s, the decade-long deficit binge had produced high interest rates, low levels of new investment, the erosion of manufacturing employment, and stagnant wages. Second, when President Bush agreed to sign the 1990 budget to begin turning things around, his party's loudest voices condemned him as betraying the Reagan Revolution and weakening the economy. The antitax climate was so intense that in his acceptance speech at the 1992 convention, the president felt compelled to say he'd made a mistake in signing the tax increase and to pledge he'd never do it again. His antigovernment wing was demanding ideological purity, even in the face of evidence that trickle-down economics defied the laws of arithmetic and no longer produced jobs. They still wanted to eat candy and never go to the dentist.

When President George W. Bush took office, it was the first time antigovernment Republicans had held both houses of Congress and the White House. They could do whatever they wanted. It soon became clear that what they wanted were big tax cuts, less regulatory oversight, and higher levels of spending. To be fair, some increased spending on national security was inevitable after 9/11. But even afterward, they cut taxes again. It was the first time the United States had ever cut taxes while waging a war. The House Republican whip, Tom DeLay, actually said that in wartime, there is nothing more important than cutting taxes.

The PAYGO rule, which had done so much to ensure fiscal discipline, was scrapped, allowing the administration and Congress to enact both big tax cuts and big increases in spending on wars in Iraq and Afghanistan, on a new prescription drug benefit for seniors, on education through the No Child Left Behind Act, and on the world's fight against AIDS and malaria through PEPFAR.

We did all this on borrowed money, increasingly from overseas, with China, Japan, the United Kingdom, Saudi Arabia, and South Korea buying the bulk of our bonds. Foreign governments now hold more of our debt than Americans do. China has more than 25 percent of the foreign holdings, at $1.2 trillion, with Japan not far behind at $900 billion.

What did we do with the money? We didn't invest it in new scientific and technological research, in rebuilding our manufacturing base, in reversing our fall from first to twelfth in the percentage of young adults with college degrees, in creating the millions of jobs that would flow from a serious response to climate change. Instead, we consumed it, in ways that distort our economy today and cloud our children's tomorrows.

From 1981 to 2009, **the greatest accomplishment of the antigovernment Republicans was not to reduce the size of the federal government but to stop paying for it.** As a result, the national debt more than quadrupled from 1981 through 1992, then doubled again between 2001 and 2009, even **before** the financial meltdown, which then required more government spending—the financial-system bailout, increased unemployment, food stamp, and Medicaid expenditures, and the stimulus—to put a floor under the downturn. At the same time, tax revenues declined as unemployment rose, businesses closed, and Americans spent less. Because interest rates are so low, it doesn't cost much more to service the increased debt today, but when the economy picks up and there's more private demand for money, interest rates will rise, and financing the debt will cost a lot more, leaving less money for investments in our future, including education, technology, research, and energy independence.

Look at these charts. They show how our debt grew from 1981 to 2011; what would have happened if the tax system and spending restraints of the 1990s

The debt crisis

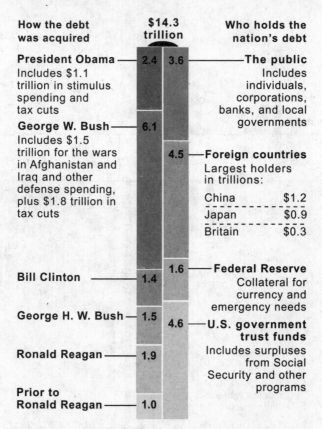

How the debt was acquired	$14.3 trillion		Who holds the nation's debt
President Obama Includes $1.1 trillion in stimulus spending and tax cuts	2.4	3.6	**The public** Includes individuals, corporations, banks, and local governments
George W. Bush Includes $1.5 trillion for the wars in Afghanistan and Iraq and other defense spending, plus $1.8 trillion in tax cuts	6.1		
		4.5	**Foreign countries** Largest holders in trillions: China $1.2 Japan $0.9 Britain $0.3
Bill Clinton	1.4	1.6	**Federal Reserve** Collateral for currency and emergency needs
George H. W. Bush	1.5	4.6	**U.S. government trust funds** Includes surpluses from Social Security and other programs
Ronald Reagan	1.9		
Prior to Ronald Reagan	1.0		

Sources: Department of the Treasury; Financial Management Service; Bureau of the Public Debt; Federal Reserve Bank of New York; Office of Management and Budget; Commerce Department; Bipartisan Policy Center.

© 2011 *New York Times*

had been maintained over the last decade, compared with what did happen when we eliminated both; and how much spending and tax cuts under President Obama have contributed to the problem compared with the policies of President Bush.

Budget Projections and Realities

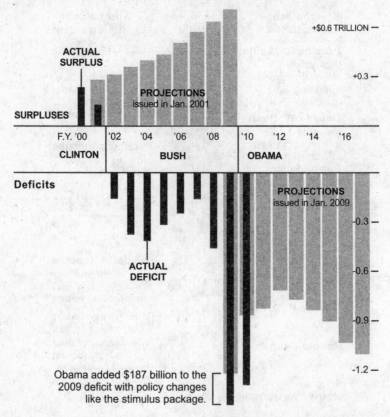

© 2011 *New York Times*

Essentially, the numbers demonstrate that after I left office, the president and Congress gave up a decade of surpluses in favor of doubling the debt. The charts also make the relentless attacks on President Obama as a big spender look a little lame when you compare the eight-year total cost of President Bush's spending and the projected eight-year cost of President Obama's initiatives. Stimulus spending will turn out about the same under both presidents.

Policy Changes Under Two Presidents
Figures in Billions

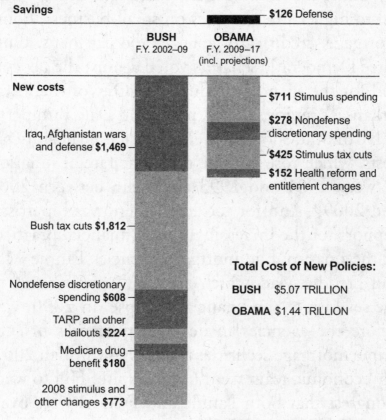

Savings

$126 Defense

	BUSH F.Y. 2002–09	OBAMA F.Y. 2009–17 (incl. projections)

New costs

Iraq, Afghanistan wars and defense **$1,469**

Bush tax cuts **$1,812**

Nondefense discretionary spending **$608**

TARP and other bailouts **$224**

Medicare drug benefit **$180**

2008 stimulus and other changes **$773**

$711 Stimulus spending

$278 Nondefense discretionary spending

$425 Stimulus tax cuts

$152 Health reform and entitlement changes

Total Cost of New Policies:

BUSH $5.07 TRILLION

OBAMA $1.44 TRILLION

© 2011 *New York Times*

All told, the combined cost of the Obama spending increases and tax cuts is about the same as the costs of the wars in Iraq and Afghanistan and almost $400 billion less than the Bush tax cuts alone.

While the decision to keep cutting taxes and spending more was driven by the antigovernment bloc that took control of the Republican Party in 1980, Democrats are not completely blameless.

Some voted for both the Reagan tax cuts and more spending in the 1980s. Back then, some liberals simply didn't think the deficits mattered, though they led to higher interest rates on small-business, home mortgage, credit card, college, and car loans. Only three Democratic senators voted against the tax cuts and for the spending reductions. One of them was Arkansas's senior senator, my friend Dale Bumpers.

No one did enough to rein in escalating health-care costs, which rose at three times the rate of inflation between 1981 and 1993 and again between 2001 and 2009.* And for too long, there was bipartisan support for the increasingly risky financial practices of the quasi-public mortgage agencies Fannie Mae and Freddie Mac, which eventually contributed to the severity of the financial collapse. In 2000, well before the agencies made large purchases of sub-prime mortgage securities from 2004 through 2007, my economic team went up to Capitol Hill to warn Congress that both Fannie and Freddie were over-leveraged. They were told by representatives of both parties, many of whom had received generous contributions from the agencies' executives, to go back to the White House.

I made some mistakes too, though not the ones I've been most widely criticized for: aggressively

---

*In the eight years of my administration, health costs increased at about the same rate as overall inflation, and we had an increase in the percentage of Americans with health insurance for the first time in twelve years.

enforcing the Community Reinvestment Act (CRA) and signing the bill repealing the Glass-Steagall Act, the Depression-era law requiring commercial and investment banking to be done by separate institutions.

Conservatives blame the CRA, which requires banks to make loans in the communities from which they take deposits, for forcing banks to make risky mortgage loans they wouldn't have made otherwise. It's true that my administration vigorously enforced the CRA requirement and that by the time I left office, more than 95 percent of the CRA loans made since the law was passed in the 1970s, more than $800 billion worth, had been made in the eight years I served. Of course, not all the CRA loans were for mortgages. Some were small-business loans, which are in short supply again today. And making mortgages available to people in the community didn't cause the meltdown. One study found that CRA–compliant banks were actually less likely to fail during the financial crisis than banks that shipped more of their deposits out of the community in hopes of getting higher returns elsewhere.

Many progressives believe the mortgage crisis was hastened and enlarged by the end of the division between commercial and investment banks. I've seen this argument in print dozens of times without supporting examples, as if it were self-evident. It isn't. Many purely commercial banks made bad mortgage loans and failed. The first bailouts went to an insurance company, AIG, and Bear Stearns, an investment bank with no commercial operations.

By the time Glass-Steagall was repealed, Federal Reserve rulings, beginning in the late 1980s, had already eliminated restraints on big banks' ability to engage in both commercial and investment banking activities, except for restrictions on underwriting insurance. The real problem was that both before and after I signed the bill, the Securities and Exchange Commission (SEC), which oversees investment banks, lacked the authority to require investment banks to set aside more cash to cover high-risk investments (though there were other steps a vigorous SEC commissioner could have taken to reduce the risks of a crash), and the bank regulators didn't do enough to limit commercial banks' risky loans.*

At any rate, now federal regulators do have the authority to limit leverage under the financial reform bill, and two big investment banks, Goldman Sachs and Morgan Stanley, have decided to become bank holding companies, and therefore subject to cash reserve requirements.

The best argument against repealing Glass-

---

*The experience of other countries proves the point. Banks in the United Kingdom, Ireland, and Iceland got in trouble without any subprime mortgage securities because they took on too much debt without adequate cash reserves. By contrast, Canada has a unified banking system that stayed strong because banks limited their risks in both commercial and investment operations.

Steagall is that it may have accelerated the speed of bank consolidations, which were already well under way, encouraging banks to get bigger, faster. Some believe that big banks are less inclined to make small-business loans than community banks.

I do think I can be fairly criticized for not making a bigger public issue out of the need to regulate financial derivatives. I couldn't have done anything about it, because the Republican Congress was hostile to all regulations, going so far as to threaten to leave the SEC with no budget because the commissioner, Arthur Levitt, was vigilant in doing his job. But I should have spoken out more, especially after Congress included a measure barring financial derivatives from being regulated as securities or commodities in an appropriations bill that passed by a veto-proof majority. In not doing so, I ignored one of my own rules: even when you can't win, it's best to get caught trying.

Brooksley Born, head of the Commodity Futures Trading Commission, did say that financial derivatives should be subject to the same kinds of capital and transparency requirements as agricultural derivatives. In 2010, her position was vindicated when Senator Blanche Lincoln, chair of the Agriculture Committee, passed an amendment to the financial reform bill to require financial derivatives to be traded more like agricultural ones. It had to be done. After I left office, the unregulated financial derivatives markets increased sevenfold in just seven years, to $700 trillion, including the newly invented vehicles that contributed to the crash. The nation's laws and regulations weren't updated until 2010.

Whatever our shortcomings, because Democrats, whether conservative, liberal, or moderate, basically believe government has an important role to play in our lives, they want it to work well. That makes most of them less ideological and more open to policies that have both progressive and conservative elements than their antigovernment adversaries.

For example, under President Reagan, the Democratic Congress actually approved slightly **less spending** than he asked for, by increasing domestic spending a little less than they reduced his requests for defense spending increases.* Under the first president Bush, they passed the PAYGO rule. When I was president, we passed the 1993 budget to reduce the deficit by $500 billion, roughly half from spending cuts, half from tax increases, with only Democratic votes. The bill produced a much greater reduction in the annual deficit than experts predicted, **eliminating roughly 90 percent of it even before the Balanced Budget bill was enacted,** because it led to lower interest rates, more investment, **and** higher growth, which brought in more revenues and reduced costs as more people got jobs and left government supports behind. Many

*See http://www.gpo.gov/fdsys/pkg/GPO-CDOC-107sdoc18/pdf/GPO-CDOC-107sdoc18-1-12-4.pdf.

Democrats voted for the welfare-reform bill after we persuaded the Republicans to restore the federal eligibility for food stamps and medical care for welfare recipients and their children. Most Democrats voted for the Balanced Budget Act of 1997 and the subsequent ones that allowed us to pay down $452 billion on the national debt.

The debt would have been reduced by even more, had it not been for the big tax cuts, spending initiatives, and brief recession in President Bush's first year in office, which included the final eight months of my last budget. If the tax rates and spending restraints of the 1990s had been kept in place, and the economic crisis had not occurred, the United States would have paid off its entire public debt by 2013 for the first time since 1832, perhaps a couple of years later because of the cost of going after al-Qaeda in Afghanistan. Even if the financial crash had happened, it would have been much easier to handle and would not have cast such a shadow over our future. And we could have financed a larger stimulus with less controversy and a smaller burden on our future.

In 1993, Democrats did raise taxes on upper-income Americans and large corporations but also cut them on lower-income working families and later, in legislation with bipartisan support, voted to cut them on middle-class parents with children, parents who adopted children, and families paying for higher education, on income from capital gains, and on investments in areas of high unemployment. We strengthened regulations to clean the air and water and ensure the safety of our food. And Al Gore's Reinventing Government initiative not only eliminated sixteen thousand pages of regulations, it also ended unnecessary programs, improved others, and changed government procurement and other practices to improve performance and save money.

Once the antigovernment bloc in Congress realized, in early 1996, that it would take another election victory to repeal the tax increases in the 1993 budget or to eliminate or severely reduce the government's role in education, economic development, health care, environmental protection, and several other areas, we worked together to reform the government's role so that it could serve the American people in the new reality of the twenty-first century.

If you look at what has actually happened in America over the last thirty years, it's clear that the idea that government is the cause of all our problems is wrong. The idea that there's no such thing as a good tax or a bad tax cut, and no such thing as a good regulation or a bad deregulation, is wrong.

So is the idea that there's no such thing as a good program or a bad program cut. For example, in 1995, the Social Security Administration (SSA), in an independent study by Dalbar Inc., was rated as having the best telephone customer service among a group of world-class companies, including FedEx, L.L.Bean, Southwest Airlines, and Disney. In 2000, SSA received recognition for its innovative and sophisticated customer service approach from **CIO** magazine as a CIO 100 honoree, the only major federal agency on the list, along with major corporations like Amazon.com, Intel, Ford Motor Company, and Marriott International. In 2011, the Veterans Administration (VA) became the first hospital system in the nation to order and implement simple, uniform sterilization procedures to prevent hospital infections, which cause tens of thousands of deaths and add tens of billions of dollars to our health-care costs every year. Though there have been a few cases of infection in VA hospitals caused by equipment not properly sterilized, the rate of infections has been reduced dramatically. Medicare and Medicaid have far lower administrative costs than private insurance companies. Led by for-profit insurance companies, our health-care system spends about eleven cents on the dollar more on paperwork and administration than any other wealthy nation. That's more than $200 billion a year.

The Federal Emergency Management Agency (FEMA), which was roundly criticized after Katrina, was probably the most popular department in the federal government during my administration because the director, James Lee Witt, had a strong background in emergency management, put together a first-rate professional staff, and instilled an ethic of speed, service, and compassion up and down the line. Ron Brown was a very highly regarded commerce secretary because he supported companies' efforts to become more productive, recognized them for doing so, and devoted the resources of his department to helping them sell more American-made products around the world. Mickey Kantor and Charlene Barshefsky were good trade representatives because they negotiated and implemented a total of three hundred new trade agreements and supported strong enforcement of the provisions of those agreements that protect American economic interests. As secretary of the interior, Bruce Babbitt was widely praised for protecting irreplace-able areas and operating a national park system that has been emulated by nations all over the world. Gov-ernment doesn't always mess everything up. It can be worth what you pay for it.

To get America back into the future business, we'll have to make choices and changes in both our gov-ernment and our private economic practices. To cre-ate jobs and raise incomes; to create new businesses and restore our manufacturing base; to have a finance sector that both earns money for itself and promotes a strong economy; to save ourselves and our chil-dren from the ravages of climate change in a way that increases growth and broadens prosperity; to move back to a balanced budget—these tasks will require the best ideas of conservatives, liberals, and moder-ates, Democrats, Republicans, and independents.

But we can't get the right answers if we begin with the wrong question. How can we weaken our gov-ernment, reduce its revenues, and restrict its reach so we can throw off its chains? That's the wrong ques-tion. We've been asking it too long.

Here are the right questions: How can we move back to a full-employment economy with good jobs and rising middle-class incomes? How can we restore American leadership for peace and prosperity and leave our children and grandchildren a brighter future? What do Americans need government to do to achieve these goals? How are we doing now, compared with our own history and expectations? How are we doing compared with the competition from other nations? As you'll see, there remains a lot of space for a real, productive debate, areas in which both Democrats and Republicans could contribute to bipartisan solutions that actually get our country back in the future business.

In a positive political environment, liberals and conservatives could learn from each other and advance the public interest. Liberals want to use the government to solve problems and are usually eager to experiment, believing, like Robert Browning's Andrea del Sarto, that "a man's reach should exceed his grasp." True conservatives are more cautious, reminding us that if something sounds too good to be true, it probably is. Liberals believe that government can solve social problems, or at least mitigate them. Conservatives believe culture, including a strong work ethic and stable families, matters more. Progressives believe they can advance liberal goals in a way that reinforces positive cultural norms and avoids "too good to be true" options. Libertarians caution against the potential of even well-conceived government initiatives to restrict individual liberty.

In the end, we need to take into account all of these perspectives to reboot and rebalance our economy. Today, our process is too tilted in favor of powerful private interests over the public interest, in favor of short-term financial gains over long-term employment and income growth, in favor of consumption over investment, in favor of pushing more of our national income up to the top 1 percent over increasing the incomes of the middle class and giving poor people a chance to work their way into it.

The only people who have taken themselves out of this needed debate are the antigovernment ideologues. They already have the answers, and the fact that the evidence doesn't support them is irrelevant. The inevitable consequence of their policies is to push the pedal to the metal of the most destructive trends of the last thirty years, to increase inequality and instability, and to forfeit the future.

CHAPTER 3

Why We Need Government

WHAT DO WE NEED A NATIONAL government for in the twenty-first century? According to the anti-government activists, not much beyond national security and trade deals. Most everything else is seen as interfering with free markets and impos-ing unnecessary taxes. For the first time since 1995, they seem determined to radically reduce the size of the federal government as much as they can until the voters stop them. After the new antigovernment majority in the House of Representatives began air-ing their budget-cutting proposals in 2011, Repre-sentative Ron Paul was asked if he favored selling off the Grand Canyon. After some hesitation, he said no, then said, "Is that a trick question?" To his credit, he didn't say yes, but he was suspicious. After all, it's a national park, the park rangers are gov-ernment employees, all paid for by our tax dollars. There must be something wrong with it.

I think the role of government is to give people the tools and create the conditions to make the most of our lives. Government should empower us to do things we need or want to do that we can only do together by pooling our resources and spending them in large enough amounts to achieve the desired objectives.

Here's a list of what that covers today:

1. **National security,** including the military, intelligence agencies, diplomatic efforts and development assistance, homeland defense, federal law enforcement, border control, natural-disaster response, and the area most recently added to the list by the Pentagon and the CIA, combating climate change.

2. **Assistance to those otherwise unable to fully support themselves and to provide a decent retirement for seniors,** including Medicaid, Medicare, and Social Security, aid for the disabled, food stamps, unemployment benefits, nutrition aid for newborns and mothers, and public housing.

3. **Equal access to opportunity,** including federal aid to education for low-income and disabled students, the HOPE Scholarship tax credits for college tuition costs, the student-loan program, Pell Grants, work-study payments, and job-training assistance.

4. **Economic development,** including trade agreements; financing for businesses to enter

new markets; incentives to create new businesses
and jobs in advanced manufacturing, clean
energy, energy efficiency, and other high-growth
areas; investments in basic research and
development and incentives for private research
and development to be done in the United
States; an adequate minimum wage and support
for work and child-rearing, including the Family
and Medical Leave law and the child tax credit;
Small Business Administration–guaranteed,
microcredit, and community development loans
to promising businesses that would otherwise be
shut out of credit markets; financing and other
support to help companies sell products made
in America in other countries; and incentives to
invest in areas of high unemployment and low
incomes.

5. **Oversight of financial markets and
institutions** to ensure transparency and honest
dealing, competition, and consumer choice and
to limit leverage to avoid future collapses and
bailouts.

6. **Protection and advancement of public
interests the market can't fix,** including clean
air, clean water, safe food, safe transportation,
safe workplaces, civil rights, access to affordable
health care, and preservation of natural resources
for the common good, including national parks,
national monuments, and national forests.

7. **Providing investments,** through tax or fee
revenue, for projects we all need when the costs

are too great or the cost recovery period too
long for the private sector to finance, including
highways, airports, rails, accelerated broadband
connections, a national electric grid, and critical
research and development in areas from space
to advanced materials to nanotechnology and
biotechnology to clean energy.

   8. **A revenue collection system,** to collect taxes
and issue credits and deductions deemed by
Congress to be in the national interest, including
tax deductions for home-mortgage payments,
charitable giving, health-care payments, children,
and many business expenses and deductions.

Now, this is a very long list, though I've left many
federal activities and programs off for the sake of
brevity. But the big ones are there. You may think
we should stop doing some of these things. Even if
you don't, there are opportunities to save money.
In 2010, Congress updated the Government Performance and Results Act of 1993, requiring the
Government Accountability Office (GAO) to identify government programs that have duplicative
activities and other areas for cost savings or revenue
increases without raising tax rates. In March 2011,
the GAO issued its report, detailing areas where several programs are doing the same things, other areas
of potential savings, and opportunities to increase
revenue through better government enforcement
and elimination of duplicative tax credits.

Partial implementation of just two of these recommendations—collecting just one-fourth of the taxes that are owed but unpaid every year, $345 billion, and putting one-third of the approximately $170 billion in no-bid contracts the government approves every year up for competitive bids—could reduce the annual deficit by more than $100 billion a year, or more than $1 trillion over a decade. Over the last fifteen years, switching from no-bid to competitive bid contracts has saved the taxpayers a lot of money, lowering their costs, on average, 25 to 30 percent. Both these changes are harder to make than they sound, but these recommendations and others in the GAO report, even if only partially implemented, could reduce the debt and actually improve performance.

We're also ripe for a review of the clarity, efficiency, and costs of federal regulation, building on the groundbreaking work Al Gore did with the Reinventing Government initiative or what Erskine Bowles did at the Small Business Administration, where he reduced loan applications from one-inch thick to one page front and back and cut the waiting time for approval from ten to three weeks. President Obama has ordered an ongoing review of regulations and has received the first set of proposed changes, which are designed to save $10 billion and to be especially helpful to small businesses. Congress, with a large bipartisan majority, has already voted to reduce the most onerous small-business reporting requirements in the health-care law.

This is all work that would save taxpayers time and money. A good conservative (or a good progressive!) could have a field day just working through the GAO report and acting on its findings.*

BUT IF YOU THINK THAT TO balance the budget, we should eliminate virtually all government departments, including the Department of Education, the Environmental Protection Agency, the Labor Department and the Occupational Safety and Health Administration, the Securities and Exchange Commission, the Commerce Department, the Energy Department, the National Institutes of Health, the National Science Foundation, the Agriculture Department, the Interior Department, and the national parks—if you're against them all, you can be a leader in the antigovernment movement's next struggle! It won't, however, make you a leader in bringing down the debt that twenty years of combining tax cuts with more spending ran up. Because that's not where the money is.

And it's not in foreign aid either. For decades, every time the American people have been asked how to balance the budget, the first thing they say is "Cut foreign aid." When asked how much of the

---

*You can find more about the specific examples of deficit reduction possibilities I mention in this chapter and many others besides in the GAO report at http://www.gao.gov/ereport/gao-11–318sp.

budget we **should** spend on foreign aid, people normally say about 10 percent. When asked how much we **do** spend, they say between 15 and 25 percent. The difference is a lot of money. The problem is that for decades our spending on foreign assistance has been around 1 percent of the budget. That's where it still is, even with substantial development spending in Afghanistan and Iraq. Almost all other wealthy countries spend a higher percentage of their budget on foreign assistance than we do. In many countries, especially in Africa, China is spending more than we are in absolute terms, building highways, rail systems, and other infrastructure projects in the hope of gaining access to Africa's metals, minerals, and other materials to fund its growth.

When he was in office, the former secretary of defense Bob Gates, a Republican, repeatedly said that an adequate foreign assistance budget for the State Department is essential to our national security, and he urged Congress not to cut foreign aid. Some of Secretary of State Clinton's most important work to build a world with more partners and fewer adversaries has involved the wise investment of relatively modest amounts of your tax money to educate and empower women and girls, fund small loans for poor people to start businesses, help developing countries secure needed energy at lower costs, and reduce the enormous toll of death and injury that results from cooking with charcoal by distributing 100 million clean cookstoves.

So what's a well-intentioned conservative to do? Actually, he or she could do a lot, hopefully with bipartisan support, if willing to take on lobbyists for private contractors—alas, also bipartisan—dedicated to protecting **the way** foreign aid is spent. Too much of the money appropriated for foreign assistance, sometimes more than 50 percent, never reaches the nations or the people it's designed to help, largely because it is channeled through U.S. contractors who take a lot of it off the top for overhead and administrative costs both in the United States and in the affected country. If we gave a higher percentage of the money to local governments with proven records of honesty, transparency, and ability, or to locally operating nongovernmental organizations with low overhead costs and proven capacity to do the job, we could educate more kids, save more lives, raise more farmers' incomes, bring clean water, decent housing, and electricity to more people, and make more friends.

In one African country where my foundation works, a U.S. contractor said it would take six months and cost $3 million to complete a project required before U.S. aid could be released to buy lifesaving drugs. Six months was too long and $3 million too much for the relatively simple project. Our people did it in six weeks for $80,000. Changing this system is a task ready-made for bipartisan reform.

But that's still not where the money is. Medicare, Medicaid, Social Security, the defense budget, and interest on the debt claim eighty-five cents of every federal tax dollar. The entire rest of the budget, called discretionary nondefense spending, claims only 15 percent. Included in that 15 percent are our investments in the future—in education, infrastructure, clean energy, research. Our quality-of-life budget is also there—in a clean environment, safe food, air traffic control, a safe workplace, and much more.

If you're an antigovernment activist who wants to do away with all this stuff, you might use the deficit as an excuse to eliminate as much of the 15 percent as you can, but you won't get rid of the deficit; you'll probably force increases in state taxes to pick up some of the activities; and you'll reduce the productivity of our workforce, our rate of economic growth, and our quality of life.

CHAPTER 4

So What About the Debt?

EVEN THOUGH OUR IMMEDIATE PRIORITY SHOULD be putting people back to work and restoring healthy economic growth, the rapid increase of our national debt over the next ten to twenty years, if not addressed, will cause us big problems. When I took office in 1993, after the debt had quadrupled since 1981, it was 49 percent of GDP.* By 2001, after four years of declining deficits followed by four budget surpluses,† total debt had dropped to 33 percent of GDP and was projected to be eliminated

*These percentages refer to the percentage of our debt held by the public and foreign governments, not the Federal Reserve's holdings and the Treasury bonds held by the Social Security and other trust funds.

†My first full budget was for fiscal year 1994, the last for fiscal year 2001, which began in October 2000 and ran through the first eight months of President Bush's first year. His tax cuts reduced the 2001 surplus but didn't eliminate it until 2002.

completely by 2013, assuming both the tax structure and PAYGO spending restraints were maintained.

From 2001 to September 2008, tax cuts, spending increases, and weak job growth (fewer taxpayers, more benefits users) doubled the debt again. Then the recession hit, and the tax relief and increased spending passed to put a floor under it, plus lower tax receipts and more people eligible for food stamps, medical benefits, and unemployment, added another $3 trillion to the debt. Now it's up to 69 percent of our GDP and rising.

Of course, when normal economic growth returns and employers start hiring again, the costs associated with surviving the recession will go down and tax revenues will increase. Nevertheless, according to the Congressional Budget Office, with the retirement of the baby boomers, the oldest of whom turn sixty-five this year, and inflation in health-care costs back with a vengeance, the debt is projected to grow to 100 percent of GDP by 2021 and almost 200 percent by 2035.

We can't let this happen. If it does, interest rates will explode, our GDP will be reduced, and our children's future will be compromised. There are only three things we can do to turn the debt problem around before it becomes a crisis: restrain spending below current projections, raise taxes, and grow the economy faster. We have to do all three. This chapter is about the first two.

As the bipartisan National Commission on Fiscal

Responsibility and Reform, usually referred to as the Simpson-Bowles Commission, has recognized, we shouldn't take a big bite out of the annual deficit and the total debt until the economy starts to grow again, but as reasonable growth returns, we do need to implement a serious long-term plan to reduce the debt. What should be in it?

A. Cutting Spending

When I was growing up, most everyone I knew was familiar with a wisecrack attributed to the famous bank robber Willie Sutton. When asked why he robbed banks, he replied, "Because that's where the money is."

In the federal budget, as mentioned earlier, the money is in Medicare, Medicaid, Social Security, the military, and interest on the debt. The only thing we can do about interest payments is to reduce our debt as a percentage of national income by growing the economy and cutting the deficit. In times of normal economic activity, the budget should be balanced or, if we want to pay the debt down to increase America's economic independence, in surplus. During recessions, deficits are almost inevitable because government income drops and, even if there's no stimulus program, spending goes up because so many people need help just to survive. Remember, in this recession as many as 15 percent of Americans have qualified for and used food stamps.

As for the defense budget, you can expect military spending, including spending on private contractors, to drop as the wars in Afghanistan and Iraq wind down. To their credit, congressional Republicans have altered their original "no defense cuts" position and agreed to the Pentagon's request to eliminate a contract to build backup engines for the new Joint Strike Fighter because the plane's manufacturer can build all the engines needed. Bipartisan support for this cut will save up to $3 billion. The Pentagon, including the Marine Corps, also wants to cancel the proposed amphibious Expeditionary Fighting Vehicle, which the corps says it doesn't need, at a savings of $9 to $10 billion. It is questionable whether we still need eleven aircraft carrier battle groups, given the likely deployments of the next several years and the fact that no other navy has more than two. The elimination of even one would save $11 billion.

THE TRICARE HEALTH PLAN, AVAILABLE TO all veterans, has a very modest enrollment fee with modest co-pays and no deductibles.* We could switch to a sliding scale based on income and raise a fair amount of money, as long as we do it without putting more burdens on veterans returning from

*See TRICARE: Summary of Beneficiary Costs, http://www .tricare.mil/tricaresmart/product.aspx?id=442.

combat with bleak job prospects or disability conditions, including post-traumatic stress disorder and other wounds sustained in service to our nation. The unemployment rate for veterans exceeds 12 percent, 25 percent above our national rate of 9 percent, and more than 200,000 veterans have head injuries, mostly from exposure to IEDs, the improvised explosive devices commonly called roadside bombs.

While defense spending can and should come down—we spend about as much as all other nations combined—we have to be careful how, when, and how much we cut it. We have to maintain enough personnel to deal with future conflicts and emergencies, without the terrible toll multiple deployments to combat zones with limited breaks in between took on military families when deployments in Iraq and Afghanistan were both at their high-water mark. We have a lot of old military equipment that has to be repaired or replaced after years of heavy use. And we don't want to cut the advanced research budget that gave us the drones, first for intelligence during my administration and then, during Presidents Bush's and Obama's terms, for surgical strikes. And we can't forget that a lot of military research eventually winds up producing applications for our civilian economy, creating new businesses and good jobs.

One of the most interesting examples of the interaction between military investments and growth in the economy can be found in Orlando, Florida. For decades the military, defense contractors, and NASA have had major operations in or near Orlando. It's also the home of Disney's and Universal's theme parks and the branch of Electronic Arts that develops sports video games. The University of Central Florida, with more than fifty thousand students, designs programs and projects to serve the needs of both the defense and the entertainment operations and to support the creation and success of the new companies and good jobs that can thrive in this environment. More than one hundred companies, from the very small to the very large, have located in Orlando to do sophisticated simulation work. Simulation helps the military to train personnel, Disney and Universal to provide exciting realistic attractions, and Electronic Arts to design engrossing video games. The military invests $5 billion a year in Orlando, money it would spend on training, information technology, and targeting systems anyway. This way, it gets better results faster and grows the economy.*

Now let's look at Social Security. Is it broke? Technically, no, but there is a cash-flow problem. It's important to understand this so we can make the right decisions about what to do.

---

*For a fuller discussion of Orlando and other areas still generating growth, more good jobs, and new businesses, and the role good government policy plays in fostering and supporting such growth "clusters," you should read William J. Holstein's excellent book, **The Next American Economy** (New York: Walker, 2011).

About 60 percent of Social Security's fifty-four million beneficiaries are eligible for the benefits based on their age; the rest are disabled or dependents and survivors of retired workers. Almost all workers pay 6.2 percent of wages into the system, as do their employers. The Tax Relief, Unemployment Insurance Reauthorization, and Job Creation Act of 2010 reduced 2011 Social Security tax rates for employees to 4.2 percent. This tax rate is currently set to return to 6.2 beginning in 2012. Benefits are progressive, in that lower-income workers receive a higher percentage of their working income in benefits than higher-income workers do. Taxes are collected on earnings up to $106,800. Those who earn more pay no Social Security taxes on the amount above that.

Social Security is a pay-as-you-go system. Until 2010, revenues collected were greater than the cost of benefits. So Social Security lent the surplus revenue to the federal government in return for Treasury Department securities worth the same amount, plus interest. The value of the Treasury bonds is more than $2.5 trillion. The interest earnings of the trust fund are greater than this year's payout, but those earnings also are paid in more bonds, not cash.

Because it is not paid in cash, the Social Security fund is nowhere near broke, yet it has begun to run a cash-flow deficit, $45 billion in 2011. That means that this year beneficiaries' checks will be funded in part from money borrowed from U.S. and overseas buyers of our bonds. The amount we borrow will continue to grow as the baby boomers move into retirement age, unless the rest of the government begins to operate with a surplus sufficient to cover Social Security's outlays or slows the projected increase in the program's cost.*

Social Security's current cash shortfall and future problems are the result of a number of factors. First, over the next eighteen years, baby boomers, born between 1946 and 1964, will turn sixty-five. We are too large a group for those in the workforce to support at present tax and benefit levels. In 1960, there were 5 workers per beneficiary. Today the ratio is 3 to 1. By 2025, there will be just 2.3 workers paying into Social Security for each beneficiary. Thankfully, the generation called the millennials is more populous than the baby boomers. As they enter the workforce and we boomers pass away, the United States will get back to a more stable worker-to-retiree ratio.

Meanwhile, we have to figure out what to do for the next thirty-five to forty years, especially since seniors are living longer, and therefore will draw more benefits than previous generations. When Social Security was inaugurated, average life expectancy was slightly below the age at which benefits began. Today, older Americans have a considerably

*Glenn Kessler, "Social Security and Its Role in the Nation's Debt," **Washington Post** online, July 12, 2011, http://www.washingtonpost .com/blogs/fact-checker/post/social-security-and-its-role-in-the -nations-debt/2011/07/11/gIQAp1Wl9H_blog.html.

longer life expectancy. American men who reach age
sixty-five have a life expectancy of eighty-two. For
women, it's eighty-four. It's a good problem to have,
one I'm trying to acquire myself, but it increases the
cost of Social Security.

Not long ago, the age for receiving full benefits
began to be raised two months each year, until it
reaches sixty-seven in 2027. That will take some
pressure off, but it won't solve the problem. The
Simpson-Bowles Commission thinks that over time
we should gradually raise the eligibility age to sixty-
nine, at least for people who don't have strenuous
jobs. The commission also advocates changing the
way we calculate annual cost-of-living increases
in Social Security payments, because the formula
now used actually increases payments more than
seniors' living expenses go up. If we do lower the
rate of benefit increases, provision will have to be
made for older people of modest means who have
health-related costs not fully covered by Medicare,
or Medicaid if they qualify for that too.

The second challenge facing Social Security is
that even though 90 percent of workers pay into
the system, the percentage of earned income subject
to the tax has dropped from its historical average
of 90 percent to 86 percent, as more and more of
the income gains for the last thirty years have gone
to higher-income Americans. The maximum wage
cap, now $106,800, has not increased as much as
wages above the cap. According to the best available

estimates, by 2020, when the cap is scheduled to be $168,000, only 83 percent of wages will be covered. Since 1980, the only time when the incomes of those in the lowest 20 percent of earners rose as much, in percentage terms, as the highest 80 percent was in the four years of my second term, thanks to a tight job market and more support for working families. Even then, the largest gains were concentrated in the top 10 percent and especially in the top 1 percent. Rising inequality is causing Social Security problems.

That's why the Simpson-Bowles Commission recommended raising the cap to $190,000 in 2020 and returning to 90 percent coverage by 2050. If we adopt that approach, the highest-income Americans, who were the biggest winners in the last decade's wage growth and tax cuts, still won't make much of a contribution to solving the problem. Some experts have suggested that a better, fairer way to raise more money is to impose a surcharge of 1 to 1.5 percent on all earnings above the cap for employers and employees.

There have been a number of Social Security reform proposals that would make the system solvent for seventy-five years, by raising the retirement age and the earnings cap, reducing the role of automatic benefit increases, and actually increasing payments to the neediest, most vulnerable beneficiaries. The Simpson-Bowles Commission plan does that. You might also want to check out the ideas of

President Obama's former Office of Management and Budget director Peter Orszag and his colleague Peter Diamond, and those of Bob Pozen, who was a member of President Bush's Social Security reform commission.*

The only sacrifice-free option that would ease but not solve the problem is to add more people to the workforce to increase monthly Social Security tax payments. The three large pools of potential new workers are seniors themselves, people with disabilities who can work, and new immigrants. In the late 1990s, I signed two bills that I hoped would encourage more workforce participation. One allowed seniors to enter the workforce without having their own Social Security payments reduced, but they would still pay income and payroll taxes on new earnings. The other allowed people with disabilities to enter the workforce without losing their Medicaid benefits. Previously, when disabled people had to give up Medicaid coverage if they took a job, very few of them could afford to work because their annual health-care costs are often greater than any salary they could earn, and they are uninsurable

*Peter Orszag and Peter Diamond, "A Summary of Saving Social Security: A Balanced Approach," May 2004, http://dspace.mit.edu/handle/1721.1/64164; Peter Orszag, "Saving Social Security," New York Times, November 3, 2010, http://opinionator.blogs.nytimes.com/2010/11/03/saving-social-security/; Robert C. Pozen, "Why My Plan to Fix Social Security Will Work," USA Today, June 12, 2005, http://www.usatoday.com/news/opinion/editorials/2005–06–12-pozen-edit_x.htm; http://bobpozen.com/.

under employer-provided policies. Now disabled Americans can enter the workforce and contribute payroll taxes to the Social Security fund.

Both Presidents Bush and Obama tried to reform our immigration laws to legalize more immigrants whose earnings would contribute to the Social Security fund. As long as we have a shortage of Americans trained in science, math, and high-tech fields, just increasing the number of well-educated immigrants under the H-1B visa program would help cutting-edge companies grow and add new employees who are American citizens to their workforce. The Obama administration announced a change in immigration policy in August 2011 that is a step in the right direction. Previously, immigrants with special skills, mostly in technology, had to have a specific job offer to get a visa. Now they are eligible if they commit to starting a new business. When they do, they and their employees will pay Social Security taxes.

Of course, these proposals are academic as long as the United States is creating so few jobs, but they're worth keeping in mind when the economy gets going again, because we need to make some changes in Social Security, and more people contributing to the system means lower burdens in future tax and benefit changes for everyone else.

The long-term health of Social Security is very important. Though most seniors have other sources of income, almost half of them would fall below the poverty line without their monthly Social Security checks. Because everyone recognizes that Social Security has a cash-flow problem, that costs are rising as the number of seniors increases, and that the available options to fix the problem are not too draconian, even the AARP has indicated a willingness to negotiate a long-term solution. If we did, it could reduce the debt by $200 billion or more over ten years.*

EVEN WITH SUBSTANTIAL REDUCTIONS below future projections in nondefense discretionary spending, and savings in the military budget and Social Security, we still won't be able to balance the budget, because of the growth of health-care spending, led by Medicare and Medicaid, but including the Children's Health Insurance Program, the Federal Employees Health Benefits Program, the VA system, and the TRICARE system for veterans. Since 1981, overall health-care costs have increased at three times the rate of inflation, although during the 1990s, the spread of managed care and the spotlight the health-care reform effort put on excessive costs kept increases closer to the overall rate of inflation. The cost restraints and the Children's Health

*The Moment of Truth: Report of the National Commission on Fiscal Responsibility and Reform (Washington, D.C.: White House, 2010), fig. 17, p. 65.

Insurance Program, enacted in 1999, led to the first increase in the percentage of Americans with health insurance in twelve years.

When the large cost increases began again in 2001, the percentage of our citizens without insurance started going up again. Every time this happens, it increases the deficit, because government spending on health care goes up. For example, in 2009, in the depths of the recession, insurance companies raised their rates so sharply that their profits increased 56 percent, while most Americans were worried about going broke. As a result, five million people lost their health coverage, and more than three million of them became eligible for Medicaid.* Ironically, the very for-profit insurance companies to which the antigovernment members of Congress want to give even more control over our health care are forcing more people into Medicaid, driving up the federal deficit the Tea Party deplores. Rising Medicaid costs also strain state governments' budgets because the states must cover a portion of Medicaid's costs under a formula that maxes out at 50 percent.

If Medicare continues to increase at the projected

---

*The same thing happened again in 2010, when another five million Americans lost their coverage at work. This time insurance companies said they had to raise rates to establish a reserve to cover the uncertain costs of complying with the health-care reform law. The policyholders should get some of that money back as insurers comply with the requirement to put 85 percent of premiums into health care, a fact that undermines the case for the big increase in the first place.

rate of inflation for the next ten years, costs in excess of the Medicare payroll tax will add $625 billion to the debt. Medicare spending as a percentage of GDP is expected to rise from 3.8 percent in 2011 to between 4.1 and 4.3 percent by 2021. The costs of Medicaid and other federally funded health programs are also projected to rise faster than inflation and increase their percentage of GDP. However, if the government's health cost increases could be kept to the overall rate of inflation, the health programs' cost would be hundreds of billions of dollars less than estimated, reducing the amount of benefit cuts or tax increases necessary to balance the budget.

How could we do that?

Medicare, like Social Security, is financed by a payroll tax, 1.45 percent. While most experts think a pension system like Social Security should be financially sound for seventy-five years, the general view is that Medicare would be sound if the fund's projected solvency is eighteen years.

When I took office in 1993, the Medicare fund was scheduled to run out of money in 1999. When I left office in January 2001, its solvency had been extended to 2025, mostly through doing a host of little things to reduce health-care inflation under the direction of Secretary of Health and Human Services Donna Shalala.

The last two serious efforts to rein in Medicare costs produced greater savings than budget authorities estimated. Both the reform legislation signed by President Reagan and the savings package I signed in 1997 produced double the projected savings. Both bills received strong bipartisan support, and afterward there was virtually no public outcry that Medicare had been "cut."

What, if any, relevance do these previous efforts have to the current Medicare debate? After another decade of health costs going up at three times the rate of inflation, plus the cost of the senior drug benefit, with the retirement of the baby boomers looming, the size of the problem is bigger. Also, the easiest savings option—cutting the reimbursement rates to Medicare Advantage providers—has already been taken, with the money going to close the doughnut hole in the senior drug program and to add a few years to the viability of the Medicare fund.

Nevertheless, because we have learned so much in the last few years about how to both reduce health-care costs and improve care, there are still lots of opportunities to save money in Medicare without cutting benefits and burdening seniors who aren't wealthy. It won't be easy, in part because changing the way health care is delivered and financed is hard to "score" in terms of budget savings. But this is by far the best way to reduce the projected cost increases, because changing the delivery and finance system will bring down the overall cost of health care, not just the cost of government-funded programs. That would help all Americans, making businesses more competitive and freeing up money for them to invest in pay raises and new growth.

Easy scoring is the surface appeal of the plan

passed by the House Republicans. It would simply give Medicare beneficiaries a voucher and let them "shop" for a private plan that best meets their needs. The government can calculate exactly how much that would cost and how much it would save compared with the projected future costs of the present system. Those who oppose the plan, including me, think it's a massive shift of costs onto seniors, because the voucher will require them to spend $6,000 or more out of pocket to keep the coverage they now receive, and it will do nothing to slow the rise in overall health-care costs. The bill's supporters say the adverse effect is overstated for two reasons: first, they believe Medicare beneficiaries will have so much collective bargaining power they'll be offered policies at prices that reduce out-of-pocket costs far below $6,000 a year; and, second, they think people on Medicare "overutilize" the system, often going to the doctor when they don't really need to, so cutting back coverage a few thousand dollars a year won't do them any harm and will save the system a lot of money.*

The big problem with the first argument is that Medicare is already less costly than private insurance. One of the big talking points for the voucher plan is that the senior drug plan, Medicare Part D, costs less than its original estimates because of com-

*Mark Schoofs and Maurice Tamman, "In Medicare's Data Trove, Clues to Curing Cost Crisis," **Wall Street Journal,** October 25, 2010.

petition among drug providers. This is probably not a good analogy for two reasons. First, there was a large increase in the availability of generic drugs after the senior drug program was enacted that was not factored into the original cost estimates. Second, the more pills you produce, the less it costs to produce one more, and the drug program created new customers for more medicine. So there was a lot of competition to provide the drugs at lower-than-expected prices to millions of new customers. By contrast, the Medicare voucher proposal just switches the same people to a different system that already costs more for the same services.

As to the second argument, let's concede that some seniors' visits to the doctor are unnecessary, and many of them could afford to pay a little for the visits they do need to prevent even higher medical expenses later and give them more healthy years. What about those who can't afford it? For them, raising out-of-pocket costs will reduce the numbers of both unnecessary and needed visits. So if seniors are asked to contribute more to the cost of their doctor visits, it has to be done carefully to avoid hurting those who don't have much flexibility in their budgets.

To get to the bottom of the Medicare riddle, we have to look at the program's role in the overall health-care system in the United States and at the innovative practices that are already lowering costs and improving quality. I know it's hard to believe we could get better health care at lower costs per person, and I don't deny for a second that those of us who have adequate coverage or can otherwise afford it can get the finest care for many severe problems, including cancer and heart disease.

For example, we rank first in the world in breast cancer survivor rates, a real tribute to the advocates who have worked tirelessly for years for better detection and treatment. And if we didn't have great people fixing heart problems, someone else would be writing this book! Still, the evidence from our own experience and that of other wealthy nations that spend a far smaller percentage of their national incomes on health care than we do and get overall results that are better than ours shows that we can do it too.

How?

Because our population is aging and older people consume, on average, more health care than younger ones, and because health-care costs are projected to continue to rise much faster than inflation, Medicare and Medicaid are projected to increase their already large percentage of the government's budget over the next decade. Yet, costly as they are, these programs are less expensive than private insurance coverage.

According to the Simpson-Bowles Commission, total costs for Medicare, Medicaid, and the Children's Health Insurance Program equaled 6 percent of GDP, or about 35 percent of total health-care spending, which is 17.6 percent of GDP. That's a lot, but it's still cheaper than the same coverage would be under private plans. For one thing, administrative costs are far lower—less than half of what private plans cost. Overall health-care spending is $35 to $40 billion lower than it would be if the government's administrative costs were equal to those of private insurance companies. Even more important, the inflation rate in the government programs, though high, has been lower than the rate of increase in private coverage. As the **New York Times** economics columnist Paul Krugman has pointed out, Medicare spending per person has increased 400 percent since 1970, while private insurance has skyrocketed 700 percent.*

You can see the problem. Medicare, Medicaid, and the Children's Health Insurance Program cost the taxpayers a lot of money and will add to our budget woes over the next decade. On the other hand, they cost less than the same services would if their beneficiaries were covered by private insurance. So privatization would either lead to more overall health spending or less coverage and its consequences.

That is why the voucher plan passed by the House of Representatives is such a bad idea. It will force seniors into a more expensive market, with more

*Paul Krugman, "Medicare Saves Money," **New York Times,** June 12, 2011.

rapidly rising prices, requiring many of them to lower their standard of living or forgo needed health care.

The Simpson-Bowles Commission took a different approach, recommending a number of cost-cutting measures and much more modest cost shifting to beneficiaries, setting a budget cap for total health spending, and urging a dramatic acceleration in implementing reforms that would both save money and improve the quality of care.

Before you roll your eyes and say that's not possible, consider these examples. First, remember the one I cited earlier of the tens of billions of dollars hospital-acquired infections add to health-care costs every year, and the very inexpensive sterilization practices that will prevent the vast majority of them if all hospitals do what the VA system has already begun to do. Second, the Geisinger medical group in northeastern Pennsylvania, with more than seven hundred doctors, promises people who enroll that if someone hospitalized under its care has to return to the hospital within ninety days of release, the group will bear the entire cost of care, with no effect on the insured's premiums or related costs. The group made the guarantee after all the doctors agreed to follow the latest "best practices" in treating every condition. The best practices are provided to all the group's doctors in a continuously updated manual. Since adoption of the best-practices model, medical errors, hospital readmissions, and costs have dropped dramatically.

Third, the Mayo Clinic pioneered a system now being adopted by other providers. To further reduce the incentives to increase revenue with unnecessary procedures, all the doctors are on salary. Therefore their incomes are unaffected by how many tests they run. As everyone knows, the quality of Mayo Clinic health care is high. But not everyone knows that the Mayo system keeps costs lower than many other providers.

Still not convinced we can save money and improve health care? Every year Pennsylvania requires hospitals to report what they charge for various services and what the results are. So far, this information has shown that there is a dramatic difference in the costs of the same procedure from hospital to hospital and no connection between the higher costs and better results. The health-care reform law requires the release of statistical information by hospitals and doctors nationwide on Medicare patients. This provision, originally supported by then senator Judd Gregg, Republican of New Hampshire, and Hillary, when she was a senator from New York, would allow the analysis of hospitals' and doctors' decisions and performance in a way that protects patient privacy but has the potential to save a lot of money and improve care. According to the Dartmouth Atlas of Health Care, more than 40 percent of Americans don't receive the best available care, and the care they do get is often needlessly expensive.

One of the most important recommendations of the Simpson-Bowles Commission is that the secre-

tary of health and human services, Kathleen Sebe-
lius, expedite testing and evaluation of promising
reforms that lower costs and improve quality and use
the leverage of Medicare and Medicaid payments to
get them universally adopted as quickly as possible.
The commission doesn't "score" the changes, but we
can estimate their potential. While the United States
spends 17.4 percent of GDP on health care, the next
most expensive system in a large, wealthy country is
France at 11.8 percent. The other wealthy countries
spend as little as 8.5 percent (Japan) of GDP. The
Netherlands has a completely private system, with
an individual mandate to buy insurance, subsidies
for low-income individuals, and an overall spending cap, a system many Republicans supported
before antigovernment activists convinced them the
mandate was an unconstitutional infringement on
Americans' freedom to get sick or have an accident
and require all the rest of us to pay for it.

To be fair to the antigovernment advocates,
there's another option: people who don't buy insurance could be denied any care they couldn't pay for.
On September 12, 2011, in a televised GOP presidential debate, Representative Ron Paul responded
to a question from Wolf Blitzer about what happens when people who don't buy insurance need
lifesaving care. He said, "That's what freedom is all
about—taking your own risks." When Blitzer asked
if society "should just let him die," many members
in the crowd cheered. Is this the America you want?

There are better and healthier ways to deal with the problem. If the United States spent 11.8 percent of GDP, the same as France does, on health care, we would save $870 billion a year, money that could go into new investment, new jobs, and pay raises.*

We can't close the whole gap by moving away from pay-for-procedure to pay-for-performance health care and cutting the excess costs of for-profit insurance companies. We also have to improve our lifestyles to stay healthier. We spend $150 billion each year just to treat diabetes and other conditions is related to obesity. A lot of people are working on that, including First Lady Michelle Obama and the Alliance for a Healthier Generation, a partnership between the American Heart Association and my foundation.

If we could close just half the gap between ourselves and our major competitors, it would cut health-care costs about $435 billion a year below what they otherwise would be, and the government's programs would cost about $140 billion less. We need to work hard on this. Remember, the Simpson-Bowles Commission proposal saves $200 billion over a decade. If we closed just 25 percent of the gap in health-care spending between the United States and other wealthy nations, it would save $700 billion, three and a half times as much.

*An examination of our health system's costs compared with other countries' was done by McKinsey & Company. You can get it at http://www.mckinsey.com/mgi/rp/healthcare/accounting_cost_healthcare.asp.

We have to achieve savings that don't erode the quality of health care or the living standards of Americans of modest means. For-profit insurance companies, with their obligations to shareholders, and medical providers, with their profits enhanced by the current pay-for-procedure system, don't have the incentives to do it.

Of course, reform-minded hospitals, non-investor-owned insurance companies, innovative health-care providers, and creative employers can make their own changes, and many are doing so. For example, more and more health-care providers are controlling costs better and improving quality with coordinated care systems. And about 15 percent of U.S. companies with five hundred or more employees have already set up on-site clinics to provide primary and preventive care to employees. They're finding it increases worker productivity and saves money on health-care costs. But if we want the United States to move as quickly as possible to more cost-effective, higher-quality health care, government will have to lead the charge, offering incentives to providers to lower delivery costs and using its market power to implement reforms that prove to be effective.

The much-derided health-care reform law is already having a positive effect. Aetna has applied to the Connecticut Insurance Department for approval to lower its rates 10 percent because of the law's requirement that 85 percent of premiums go to pay for health care, not to profits and marketing. In 2012 the price for Medicare Advantage plans will drop 4 percent, and the costs of buying drugs will be flat.

So where does all this leave us with the debt? The Simpson-Bowles Commission says that if nothing changes in the way we now tax and spend, the return of normal economic growth will give us more revenues and lower costs for unemployment-related expenses. Today our annual spending is about 24 percent of GDP, and we're taxing at 15 percent, the lowest percentage in sixty years. If we had normal growth of 2.5 to 3 percent, the numbers would be more like 22 and 17 percent, leaving us with a "structural" deficit of $650 to $700 billion a year, not $1.2 trillion.

Unfortunately, over the next few years, the deficit reductions brought by the return of normal growth will be more than offset by dramatic increases in annual outlays for Social Security and health care, and over the decade, a fourfold increase in interest payments on the debt. These factors are projected to increase the debt another $9.5 trillion by 2020.

The Simpson-Bowles Commission recommended shaving $4 trillion off that over the next decade by reducing spending by $3 trillion, with more than two-thirds coming from discretionary cuts and reduced interest payments on the debt, less than a third from Social Security, health, and other mandatory programs. The other $1 trillion in debt reduction in the commission plan comes from new tax revenues.

If you assume that we could get another $1 to $1.5 trillion over ten years by making health-care delivery changes and implementing more of the GAO report's recommendations (most people don't think we can, but I do) and that if the anti-tax forces prevail in preventing any new revenue, the debt could **still** increase another $5 trillion by 2020, and the budget couldn't be balanced. Even with new revenues, the Simpson-Bowles Commission plan doesn't balance it until 2035.

Also, the big cuts in discretionary spending may well not be achievable, and in some areas would be a big mistake. Even before the budget agreement, defense was projected to be 15 percent of the federal budget by 2016, the lowest percentage since the onset of the Cold War. Much more troubling is that our **nondefense discretionary spending will fall to its lowest level as a percentage of the overall economy since 1960.** That's hardly good news if you agree that nondefense discretionary spending, investments in education, infrastructure, clean air and water, are critical to our future growth and our quality of life.

In Chapter 3, I mentioned some of the discretionary cuts in the GAO report that we should make, but a good portion of that money should be reinvested by the government to further increase our economic productivity, our quality of life, and

America's impact beyond our borders. First, for our own national security, we should be making larger, not smaller, investments across the world to reduce poverty, improve health and education, and advance freedom and democracy. Our military leaders, including Admiral Michael Mullen, the recently retired chairman of the Joint Chiefs of Staff, often remind us that making friends is cheaper than fighting wars. The politicians like to cut foreign aid, as I said earlier, because Americans think we spend a lot more on it than we do, and, unlike Medicare or farm supports, those who get it don't vote here. Second, the defense cuts are pretty steep unless the Pentagon fully implements the GAO recommendations, gets a better deal on the huge number of contracts it signs every year, and becomes more energy efficient and less dependent on imported oil. It'll do a better job of implementing these changes if it knows it can keep at least some of the money it saves to meet legitimate security needs. Even though we are winding down our involvement in Iraq and Afghanistan we can't assume we won't be involved in other conflicts in the future.

Third, and most important to our daily lives, if we're going to stay ahead of our wealthy competitors and rapidly growing nations like China, India, and Brazil, we're going to have to invest more in twenty-first-century infrastructure—in faster broadband, a modern national electrical grid, more well-distributed clean-power generation, modernized water and sewer systems, ports and airports, trains, roads, and bridges. We'll have to do a better job of educating and training a higher percentage of our people to fill the best jobs. Finally, we'll have to redouble our efforts to remain the world's best center of innovation by making continuous investments in scientific and technological research and development and by providing the infrastructure and incentives for private companies to do the same in the United States rather than some other nation.

B. More Tax Revenues

That means we can't cut the debt substantially, much less balance the budget in a reasonable time frame, without raising more revenue. The Simpson-Bowles Commission recommended lowering the corporate tax rate and eliminating most of the deductions and credits that allow many very profitable companies to avoid a large percentage of the taxes they would otherwise pay, while others pay the legal maximum of 35 percent. The 35 percent rate is now second-highest among wealthy nations, but the actual amount paid on corporate income is 23 percent, ranking us in the middle. We can raise the same amount of money or more with lower rates applied more fairly to all corporations. For example, with oil prices so high and the oil companies making record profits, we could reduce the deficit $4 billion this year alone and an estimated $77 billion over the coming decade by eliminating their tax advantages. ExxonMobil, with a second-quarter profit of $10.7 billion, has an effective tax rate of 17.6 percent, well below both the average American's rate of 20.4 percent* and the average corporate tax "take" of 23 to 25 percent.

The simplest way to generate more revenue from personal income taxes is to let the Bush tax cuts on upper-income and wealthy Americans expire in 2013. They will do so automatically if not renewed. This would raise $700 billion over a decade, more than half of it from the wealthiest 10 percent of Americans, who reaped 90 percent of the income gains in the last decade and got the large tax cuts on top of that. This is not class warfare but a reflection of our values of fairness and shared responsibilities, asking those of us who benefited from an economy that left most Americans standing still or falling behind to help put our country back on the right track to the future.

If we wanted the economic independence and strength an earlier balanced budget would bring, and the economic benefits smart, targeted investments would generate, we could restore the tax rates of the 1990s to everyone. That would net about $3.5 trillion over a decade. Of course, the anti-taxers would howl that it would be the largest tax hike in

*See   http://www.americanprogress.org/issues/2011/05/tax_man .html.

history. But in the 1990s, with unemployment low, incomes rising, and poverty declining, most Americans seemed pretty happy with a budget surplus and increased investments to keep the economy growing.

The Simpson-Bowles Commission recommended that we also lower personal rates but collect more money by restructuring and limiting the availability of credits and deductions claimed by wealthier Americans. Under its plan, instead of six rates, there would be three, at 12 percent, 22 percent, and 28 percent, with tax breaks targeted more tightly to people who need them. For example, the mortgage-interest deduction would be capped at $500,000, not $1 million. The child tax credit, employer-provided health insurance deduction, provisions governing charitable gifts, retirement savings, and pensions, and the Earned Income Tax Credit for lower-income working families would be maintained. The commission plan would require that any new deductions, or additional breaks, like a lower capital-gains rate or the tax credit for research and development (which I favor), be paid for by higher rates.

There are many other variations on these proposals ripe for debate, but the arithmetic is inescapable: we can't get the debt and interest payments on it down to a manageable level, much less balance the budget, without more revenues. The trick is to do it in a way that is fair, without rates that are high enough to encourage the flight of taxable income to other countries.

The most comprehensive alternative to the budgets passed by the House Republicans and recommended by the Simpson-Bowles Commission is the budget plan of the Congressional Progressive Caucus. It proposes to balance the budget in just ten years with an array of tax increases on upper-income Americans, especially those with incomes over $1 million a year; on estates, with steeper increases on those worth more than $50 million; on capital gains (taxing them at ordinary income rates); on corporate income; and on complex financial transactions. It would also cap standard deductions at the 28 percent rate for those in higher brackets, eliminate tax preferences for oil, gas, and coal companies, and index the alternative minimum tax to inflation. Their changes are projected to raise about $4 trillion over a decade.

On Social Security, their proposal would raise the maximum taxable limit to 90 percent of employee earnings now, not in 2020 as in the Simpson-Bowles plan, and eliminate the cap altogether for employers. On Medicare and other health programs, it keeps the president's budget savings, adds a public option to the health-reform plan to hold down overall costs, and calls for more negotiated price discounts on government health programs' high-volume drug purchases from pharmaceutical companies. Beyond health care, all the spending reductions are in the military budget, $1.8 trillion over ten years.

The third part of the progressives' plan calls for

investing more money in programs designed to create jobs and raise incomes: almost $1.5 trillion in an infrastructure bank to finance both traditional projects and new ones like faster broadband connections, a modern electric grid, and building retrofits; more funds for environmental conservation and community economic development; higher investments in education, job training, and special help for veterans and the long-term unemployed; and more spending for housing, rental, and child-care programs for lower-income Americans.

The bottom line on the progressives' budget plan is that it produces a balanced budget in ten years with deficit reduction of $5.6 trillion, comprising revenue increases of $3.9 trillion, net spending cuts of $869 billion, and interest savings of $856 billion. There are lots of obvious objections to it from those with different perspectives. Seventy percent of the gap is closed with taxes, only 30 percent with spending restraint. It would enact the highest taxes in fifty years on very wealthy Americans. Its corporate tax proposals are so at variance with even our high-tax competitors that multinationals may be tempted to relocate to other countries. Depending on the tax rates and how they're structured, the financial-transactions tax could either bring in a lot of money or lead to many high-dollar transactions now done in the United States being moved overseas, with a net loss in revenue from the taxable incomes on the people who do the transactions. And the progressives' plan doesn't deal with the demographic challenges to Social Security and the health-inflation challenges of Medicare, Medicaid, and other government-funded health programs.

Of course, in this Congress, progressives don't have the votes to pass their plan. But the plan does two things far better than the antigovernment budget passed by the House: it takes care of older Americans and others who need help; and much more than the House plan, or the Simpson-Bowles plan, it invests a lot of our tax money to get America back in the future business. That makes its specifics worth studying for possible changes and inclusion in a plan with more balance between spending restraint and new taxes.

To sum up, we have a debt problem that will get worse if we do nothing. Increasingly, the debt is being financed by other nations buying our bonds. Most of the responsibility for the debt that has already piled up lies with the antigovernment leaders who supported both big tax cuts and spending increases and, in the last decade, provided lax oversight of financial institutions that were too highly leveraged. Most of the increased spending and tax cuts under President Obama were designed to help America weather the crash. Because they are time limited, they won't contribute much to the long-term problem. The health-care bill will cost more in tax money, but overall health-care spending will be lower than it would have been without

it. And the government's costs will be less than projected if health-care cost inflation can be reduced,
a step that also will keep health costs lower for
everyone.

In contrast to the main debt drivers in the past
thirty years, tax cuts and national security spending,
most of the increase in debt over the next thirty years
will come from much more spending on programs
progressives support as forthrightly as the antigovernment forces back tax cuts for higher-income
Americans: Social Security, Medicare, Medicaid, and
other health programs. That means that if Democrats want to both preserve the programs and restore
economic growth, they have to develop a plan to
reduce their projected costs and to increase investments and tax incentives in areas vital to a quicker
economic recovery and to our long-term prosperity.
The arithmetic trumps ideology.

We have three choices on the debt. We can live
with it, with higher interest rates, slower growth,
lower incomes, less economic independence, and
the loss of our global leadership. Or we can do
what the antigovernment forces want, attacking
the problem with spending cuts only, drastically
reducing the federal government's role in providing for future growth through education, research
and development, modern infrastructure, and economic development; for a better quality of life in
clean air and safe air travel, health-care and income
security for the elderly; and for America's contin-

ued world leadership. If we do that, we'll lower our future economic growth, increase poverty and our already high level of income inequality, reduce our quality of life, and force other countries into alliances with nations that may not share our values and interests. Or we can act to strengthen both the economy and the government's role in creating a better future by cutting spending and raising revenue in a fair, effective way. That's what the president and most Democrats want to do. That is the course I favor. According to most polls, a big majority of Americans favor it too.

If you're an antitax absolutist like Grover Norquist, who works hard to get every candidate for Congress and the presidency to sign a pledge never to raise taxes, this kind of approach, indeed the idea of any more taxes, is heresy. There's only one way taxes can go—down. That means we can't cut oil-company tax breaks to finance energy independence with homegrown resources and new technologies. It means Congress can never decide that it's not right for a successful hedge fund manager's ordinary income to be taxed at the 15 percent capital gains rate, a lower rate than the fund's secretaries and other nonprofessional staff pay.* This makes sense if you think all government activity is harmful and the United

---

*A lot of the manager's income is now taxed at the 15 percent capital gains rate, though the income comes not from risking the manager's own money on investments, but is a fixed percentage of profits earned on capital the manager's investors risked.

States would do better with a philosophy grounded in "you're on your own" rather than "we're all in this together."

Before we get to the most urgent topic—how the United States can get out of the current crisis, create more jobs quickly, and lay the foundation for long-term prosperity—let's look at where we are today compared with our recent past and compared with our wealthy competitors. After all, we've been going down the antigovernment road for thirty-one years now, except for my two terms and President Obama's first two years. Let's see what the evidence shows us about how that "on your own" strategy is working for us and look at how other nations with very different policies are doing.

CHAPTER 5

How Are We Doing Compared with Our Own Past and with Today's Competition?

THE MOST SUCCESSFUL NATIONS IN THE twenty-first century have both a strong economy and a strong, effective government. To make this case, which is one of the main points of this little book, I'll have to persuade you to look at how the United States is doing compared with our own history and expectations and at how we're doing compared with other countries that are our competitors for the future, both those that are already wealthy and those that are rapidly rising. Believe it or not, you'll see that quite a few are outperforming us in terms of education, technology, modern infrastructure, research and development, and high-end manu-facturing. Many have lower unemployment rates, faster job growth, less income inequality, and lower poverty rates. Some even do a better job of giving their poor people a chance to work their way up the economic ladder into the middle class, the journey we know as the American Dream.

For example, Singapore, an island nation of just five million people, with a high per capita income and a relatively low tax burden, is making a $3 billion investment of government funds, much more than we are, to become the world's leading biotechnology center. Biotech is expected to produce new products that will create millions of jobs in the next decade. In the past decade, Germany, where the sun shines on average as much as it does in London, soared past the United States to become the world's leading nation in the production and use of photovoltaic cells.* How? With government subsidies and targets. A study by Deutsche Bank found that even allowing for the costs of the economic subsidy, the Germans had a net gain of 300,000 new jobs. Based on our much larger population, if we had adopted Germany's policy, we would have produced more than one million jobs. If you take into account our greater capacity to generate solar power, we could have created twice that many.

Let's begin with a look inward, comparing where we are now with our performance in the last half

---

*China has now surpassed Germany in the production, though not in the deployment, of solar cells.

of the twentieth century. After World War II until 1980, the bottom 90 percent of Americans consistently earned about 65 percent of the national income, and the top 10 percent earned about 35 percent, of which 10 percent went to the top 1 percent. That was enough income inequality to reward good ideas, successful entrepreneurs, and the best CEOs and enough equality to build the world's largest middle class and give hardworking poor people a chance to work their way into it. From 1981 to 2010, these numbers changed a lot, as the bottom 90 percent's income share fell from 65 to 52 percent, and the top 10 percent's rose from 35 to 48 percent, with almost all those gains going to the top 1 percent, whose income share increased from 10 percent to more than 21 percent. For the first seven years of the last decade, as median income decreased, the top 1 percent claimed around 60 percent of the gains. How did that happen?

Things began to change in the 1970s, as the United States faced more foreign competition from lower-wage nations in basic manufacturing, from Japan in consumer electronics and automobiles and from Germany in sophisticated machinery. The oil embargo led to a surge in the price of oil and other petroleum-based products, increased inflation, and further weakened jobs and depressed salary increases in the manufacturing sector, as did the decline in union membership among private-sector workers. Slow growth with high inflation, called stagflation, along with the Iran hostage crisis, helped Ronald Reagan defeat President Carter and ushered in chapter one of the antigovernment era.

In the early 1980s, the inflation threat ebbed, thanks to the stern policies of the Federal Reserve chairman, Paul Volcker; increased productivity resulting in part from the deregulation initiatives of Presidents Carter and Reagan; and the large infusion of low-cost consumer goods from overseas. By 1983, with the majority of President Reagan's tax cuts in place and a big buildup in defense spending under way, we were into permanent deficit spending, an ongoing stimulus that was reinforced by the growing reliance of consumers on credit purchases. Meanwhile, manufacturing, facing stiff competition, grew more productive, meaning fewer workers were required to produce the same output, and the United States didn't generate new manufacturing jobs by increasing exports of new high-end products. So more of our new jobs were coming in the service sector, where wages and benefits in general are lower than in manufacturing.

In the 1980s, Wall Street and many large corporations embraced what was then a new idea—that publicly traded companies' first and overwhelming obligation is to their shareholders. Until that time, most people thought a corporation, which receives limited liability and other privileges under the law, owed an obligation to all its stakeholders, including shareholders, employees, customers, and the communities of which they are a part. This "shareholders first" philosophy created an ironic situation: A corporation was now supposed to be run primarily for the benefit of the shareholders, who have the biggest interest in its short-term profits but the smallest stake in its long-term success.

This approach has continued unchecked, amplified by the dramatic rise in executive compensation based more on short-term stock appreciation than long-term viability and by an even more explosive increase in funds dedicated to complex financial transactions. These deals generate huge incomes for those who put them together and for CEOs whose companies get a bump in stock prices, but they rarely create jobs for or raise the incomes of ordinary Americans.

Over the last thirty years, this "financialization" of the American economy, combined with the antigovernment tax cuts, weaker oversight of everything from banks to polluters, and, in the last decade, lax enforcement of our trade agreements, has created a "you're on your own" economic and social policy that is the bedrock of antigovernment governance.*

---

*This is not an oxymoron. Though they profess a hatred of government, they spend lots of time and money to get control of it. In 2011, fourteen states in which Republicans held governorships and legislative majorities imposed new restrictions on voting rights, including photo ID requirements, restrictions on voter-registration drives, the elimination of election-day registration, and fewer days of early voting. According to the Brennan Center for Justice at New York University these new laws and executive orders could "make it especially harder for more than five million eligible voters to cast ballots in 2012," most of them young, minority, disabled, low income,

This approach has continued to increase the percentage of GDP claimed by the financial sector and to concentrate income gains among already wealthy Americans. It has helped a considerable number of people become millionaires and billionaires, but it has led to stagnant wages for almost everyone else. When the market is rising, it does provide substantial returns to many other Americans through their own investments and those made by retirement, mutual, and other funds, but it's been lousy for job growth.

Look at the following charts, showing the numbers of jobs created and the growth in national income since 1953. The 1960s performance was the best, followed by my two terms. President Reagan had the third-highest number of jobs, as he began America's big experiment with trickle-down economics and permanent deficits, but the steam ran out under President George H. W. Bush for all but upper-income Americans, as the big deficits led to higher interest rates and slower growth. All along, middle-class incomes were barely rising, and only 70,000 people moved from poverty to the middle class from 1981 to 1993, compared with 7.7 million in the following eight years.

Meanwhile, incomes on Wall Street and in executive suites of large corporations began their three-

---

and elderly. My favorite is Texas' new law that accepts as proof of identity a concealed-weapons permit, but not a University of Texas student's college ID card.

Job creation by term

President	Term	Number of jobs beginning of term (in thousands)	Number of jobs conclusion of term (in thousands)	Number of jobs created (in thousands)	Annual average increase
Dwight Eisenhower	1953–1957	49,470	52,168	2,698	1.4%
Dwight Eisenhower	1957–1961	52,168	52,780	612	0.3%
Kennedy/Johnson	1961–1965	52,780	58,561	5,781	2.7%
Lyndon Johnson	1965–1969	58,561	68,494	9,933	4.2%
Richard Nixon	1969–1973	68,494	74,613	6,119	2.2%
Nixon/Ford	1973–1977	74,613	79,540	4,927	1.7%
Jimmy Carter	1977–1981	79,540	89,831	10,291	3.2%
Ronald Reagan	1981–1985	89,831	95,029	5,198	1.4%
Ronald Reagan	1985–1989	95,029	105,708	10,679	2.8%
George H. W. Bush	1989–1993	105,708	108,021	2,313	0.5%
Bill Clinton	1993–1997	108,021	119,269	11,248	2.6%
Bill Clinton	1997–2001	119,269	130,433	11,164	2.3%
George W. Bush	2001–2005	130,433	130,369	-64	0.0%
George W. Bush	2005–2009	130,369	131,555	1,186	0.2%

Data reflect the number of people employed at the end of January in the year each president took office through the end of January when the president's term ended.

Source: Bureau of Labor Employment, Hours, and Earnings from the Current Employment Statistics survey (National)

GDP growth since 1955 by president

George W. Bush	1.6%
George H. W. Bush	2.1%
Gerald Ford	2.2%
Dwight Eisenhower	2.5%
Richard Nixon	3.0%
Jimmy Carter	3.2%
Ronald Reagan	3.5%
Bill Clinton	3.8%
Lyndon B. Johnson	5.0%
John F. Kennedy	5.4%

Source: *New York Times*
July 29, 2011

decade explosion. For example, in the 1960s, when our economy enjoyed its most rapid rate of growth since World War II, CEO pay in large corporations averaged 25 times that of the average worker. In the last decade, after executive compensation at our largest companies had quadrupled since 1970, the ratio rose to more than 400 times average worker pay before the financial crisis, when it fell back to 300 to 1 because so much executive compensation is tied to stock prices. It's already rebounded to almost 350 to 1, even though unemployment remains high and most Americans' incomes are stagnant or declining.

One of the best characteristics of Americans is that most of us applaud, not resent, the success of other people, as long as it's fairly earned. But we've all read stories of the golden parachutes that bestow millions on CEOs who leave companies in worse shape than they found them. Or stories about companies that have to be downsized to cut costs enough to cover debt payments for buyouts that made a killing for those who did the deal but cost workers jobs or years without pay raises even though they had helped make their company profitable before it was brought low by new debt.

The 2010 filings of 483 companies in the S&P 500 show that their 2,591 executives in total received $14.3 billion in compensation, an average of $5.5 million. Median CEO pay at large corporations was $10.8 million, which is less than it was before the recession. But in 2009 and 2010, 179 companies in the S&P 500 raised executives' pay even as the value of their shareholders' stakes fell. Meanwhile, the average American worker took home $752 a week, an increase of one-half of 1 percent, which, after inflation, was a decrease in real income.

In spite of these examples, and the well-known tales of enrichment through illegal conduct at Enron, Tyco, and others, I think most Americans respect people like Steve Jobs, who made a fortune producing products or services they want to buy like the iPad and the iPhone (though we wish they were made in the United States). And most Americans cheer the success of the many U.S. companies that have retained the loyalty of their employees and the communities of which they are a part by being loyal to them. Corning, Coca-Cola, Dow Chemical, Procter & Gamble, Starbucks, and many, many others have enjoyed financial success by making good products, providing good services, and maximizing U.S. employment and community involvement, even as their operations spread across the globe.

When I was governor of Arkansas, I helped to recruit a Nucor steel plant to the economically distressed northeast corner of our state. The company made rolled steel there. Its employees earned a modest wage but received weekly bonuses based on company profits. The bonuses usually doubled earnings, putting its workers among the highest paid in our state. In addition, the employees received an education bonus of $1,500 per year for every child they had in college. The company also had a strict no-layoff policy, which meant that if income declined, the employees' bonuses would be reduced across the board. It happened once, in a very bad year for manufacturing in the mid-1980s. The chairman and founder of the company, Ken Iverson, sent a letter to every employee, explaining that business was down 20 percent, so everyone's bonus would be reduced by that amount, but no one would be laid off. Then he said that since he hadn't succeeded in finding a way to keep Nucor growing in the face of a global downturn, he was cutting his pay by 60 percent.

Fast-forward to 2009, when Nucor actually lost money for the first time. Still, no one was laid off. Employees' hours and pay were reduced, but benefits were maintained, including the now $3,000 per child for college tuition, plus supplements to help pay the college expenses of the employees themselves and their spouses. In the toughest times, the company's culture held fast to the values of its founder. Ken Iverson was a good Republican who believed in shared benefits and shared responsibilities. We need more executives like him.

There are more than you might think. On September 11, 2001, Jimmy Dunne was one of three men who led a small investment banking firm, Sandler O'Neill & Partners, L.P., with offices on the 104th floor of the South Tower of the World Trade Center. When the second terrorist plane turned the South Tower into an inferno and brought it down, Sandler

O'Neill lost 66 of its 171 employees, including the other two men who ran the firm with Dunne. Dunne was determined both to save the firm and, in spite of its dire financial straits, to do right by the families of his lost employees. In 2001, the firm paid the lost partners' capital to their families, paid the year's remaining salaries, and awarded bonuses to fallen employees' families equal to or greater than the amount earned in their best year. It offered full benefits to all of the families for five years, then later extended them for another five, and set up a foundation to fund the education costs of the seventy-four children who lost a parent. Today, Sandler O'Neill has 340 employees and partners, including 57 of the 105 who survived, another shining example of the positive economic and employment rewards of a company that values long-term loyalty, shared benefits, and shared responsibilities.

Several other firms that lost people on 9/11 also made a real effort to take care of their families and the surviving employees who needed help. The hardest hit was the large bond-trading firm Cantor Fitzgerald, which lost 658 of its 950 employees. The company gave 25 percent of its profits to the families of its slain employees and provided for their health insurance for a decade. Now BGC, a trading arm of Cantor Fitzgerald, has an annual Charity Day on which it donates all the day's income to good causes, including those that benefit men and women wounded in military service. Another trading company, ICAP, does the same thing. For every person on Wall Street who resembles the character Michael Douglas played in the **Wall Street** movies, there are many others who give lots of money every year to increase educational and economic opportunities for poor kids and inner-city entrepreneurs.

Most of these people are grateful for their success and know that because of current economic circumstances, they're in the best position to contribute to solving our long-term debt problem and to making the investments necessary to restore our economic vitality. Many of them supported me when I raised their taxes in 1993, because I didn't attack them for their success. I simply asked them, as the primary beneficiaries of the 1980s growth and tax cuts, to help us balance our budget and invest in our future by creating more jobs and higher incomes for other people. They're smart enough to know that they can't continue to prosper on the escalator of our increasing inequality without fundamentally weakening America and killing the goose that laid their golden eggs.

Of course, there are also a lot of other people who've done well, think they were entitled to all the tax cuts, and see no connection between the concentration of income and wealth at the top, the decline of both middle-class and low-income workers, and the jobless growth pattern of the last decade.

Some of them are bankrolling the antigovernment crowd. That helps to explain some of the positions its members of Congress have taken that seem inconsistent with their rhetoric. For example, the antigovernment members of Congress railed against the financial bailout, but they support repeal of the financial-reform bill, thereby stripping government regulators of their power to make banks hold more capital to cover higher risks, increasing the likelihood of future financial failures. The bill also bars future bailouts and establishes a procedure for orderly bankruptcy instead. They want to repeal that too.

Here is a different example of a Tea Party move that at first seems consistent with its antigovernment philosophy but is really about abusing a government program with weak oversight. In August 2011, a Tea Party freshman, Representative Austin Scott of Georgia, president of the House Republicans' freshman class, introduced a bill to abolish the Legal Services Corporation. He said that poor people didn't need government-funded attorneys because they could find representation elsewhere. He said he was just trying to save the taxpayers money. The bill was introduced three days after Legal Services lawyers won a decision from the Equal Employment Opportunity Commission that Hamilton Growers, a company in Scott's district, had illegally discriminated against its U.S. workers in favor of Mexican migrant workers. The discrimination included deliberately giving the U.S. workers less favorable assignments and fewer work hours and engaging in a pattern of firing U.S. workers in order to hire more guest workers from Mexico, under a visa program that allows employers to hire them when they anticipate a shortage of American workers. The program was not set up to provide a way for employers to dismiss or refuse to hire American workers so that they can hire foreign workers at substandard wages with no benefits. The real purpose of the first bill Representative Scott sponsored was to punish Legal Services lawyers for exposing these abuses of the visa program by an employer in his district.

Ironically, in his successful 2010 campaign against a moderate Democratic incumbent, Scott promised to be tough on illegal foreign workers taking precious U.S. jobs. Though in this incident the foreign workers were technically here legally, it is still hard to see how kicking American citizens out of jobs to hire temporary immigrants is a good thing. As the **Washington Post** columnist Dana Milbank says, the Tea Party may have started as a populist revolt, "but it has been hijacked by plutocrats."*

When the Tea Party first emerged, I admired its founders' principles even when I disagreed with their policies. The early organizers were protesting a government that bailed out banks instead of holding them accountable for their unwise mortgage gambles and helped underwater home-owners

---

*Dana Milbank, "How Rep. Austin Scott Betrayed His Tea Party Roots," **Washington Post**, August 9, 2011.

who shouldn't have taken on subprime, variable-rate mortgages in the first place. They also opposed the federal legislation to aid and restructure the auto industry, believing that American companies should live with the consequences of past mistakes. I disagreed with all these positions because I thought the failure of our financial system, the lingering home-mortgage debacle, and the loss of America's ability to make cars and trucks would hurt tens of millions of hardworking, responsible citizens who had not contributed to our problems. Still, I admired the original Tea Party activists' call for more responsibility in America from top to bottom. It was sad to see the movement morph into one that kept the rhetoric of accountability but applied it only to the middle class and the working poor. Now too many foot soldiers in the antigovernment brigade are fighting for policies that protect their financial backers, promote inequality, punish hardworking middle-class Americans, increase poverty, and prevent the restoration of a strong economy.

The antigovernment movement's most cherished conviction is that we can't raise taxes on the "job creators." And not just while the economy is weak—**not ever.** Indeed, if it were up to them, they would cut taxes on high-income Americans even more, as they pledged to do in the 2010 campaign, and use the revenue shortfall as a reason to eliminate even more of the federal government than they have proposed to do in 2011.

The biggest problem with their argument is that we tried it their way for twenty of the last thirty years, and their strategy of using blanket tax cuts for high-income individuals didn't work. In these twenty years, average job growth was under one million per year, income inequality increased dramatically, more people fell from the middle class back into poverty, and more middle-class people with nonexistent pay raises kept up with inflation by maxing out their credit cards and taking second mortgages on their homes, until household debt exceeded 125 percent of income.

The Tea Party retort, of course, is that past Republican presidents and members of Congress were committed to cutting taxes and weakening regulation but weren't really serious about cutting spending. They say they **are** serious about it and that will make all the difference. They're right about that. They are serious about it, and if their policies prevail, it will make a difference. It will make things worse.

To see why, let's look at the impact that weak job growth, growing inequality, more money flowing to financial transactions that don't create growth and jobs, and less public **and** private investment in our long-term economic success have already had. We can do that by comparing how America stacks up against our major competitors today, and how those nations' policies compare with what the antigovernment ideologues advocate.

The first chart shows how we're doing in various economic and quality-of-life measures compared with other countries that the International Monetary Fund classifies as "advanced." There are thirty-three of them. Many are small, like Cyprus and Malta. Some are in deep economic trouble, like Greece. None of the rapidly rising countries like China, India, Brazil, and Russia are on the list yet, because their per capita income isn't high enough. But the rest of our serious competitors for the future are covered.

The first column measures income inequality. We rank third, with only Singapore and Hong Kong having a more unequal distribution of income. Sweden, Norway, Austria, Germany, Denmark, and Finland have the most equal income distribution, along with a couple of smaller economies.

On unemployment, the United States, at 9 percent, ranks eighth highest, with a lower rate than Spain, claiming by far the highest rate at 20 percent, followed by Slovakia, Greece, Portugal, Slovenia, France (9.5 percent), and the Czech Republic. The lowest unemployment rate is Singapore's at 2.3 percent, followed by Norway (3.7 percent), Denmark (4.2 percent), Australia (5.1 percent), the Netherlands (5.5 percent), Germany (7.1 percent), the United Kingdom (7.9 percent), Finland (7.9 percent), and Sweden (8.3 percent). The difference between these nations and the United States might be greater than the numbers indicate, because in the United States you're only counted as unemployed

American shame

How the International Monetary Fund's "Advanced Economy" countries compare on various measures.

Best — Worst — Worst of the worst

	Income Inequality (Gini Index) Higher numbers represent more income inequality	Unemployment Rate Most recent estimates	Level of Democracy (Scale of 1 to 10)	Gallup Global Wellbeing Index (percentage thriving, 2010)	Food Insecurity "Have there been times in the past 12 months when you did not have enough money to buy food that you or your family needed? Percentage answering yes.	Life Expectancy at Birth	Prison Population per 100,000 citizens	Math Scale Score	Science Scale Score
Australia	30.5	5.1	9.22	62		81.72	133	514	527
Canada	32.1	8.0	9.08	62	8	81.29	117	527	529
Norway	25.0	3.7	9.8	69		80.08	71	498	500
Netherlands	30.9	5.5	8.99	68		79.55	94	526	522
Germany	27.0	7.1	8.38	43	6	79.41	85	513	520
Austria	26.0	4.6	8.49	57		79.65	103	496	497
Switzerland	33.7	3.9	9.09	62	4	80.97	79	534	517
Denmark	29.0	4.2	9.52	82	3	78.47	71	503	499
Finland	29.5	7.9	9.19	75		79.13	60	541	554
Belgium	28.0	8.1	8.05	56		79.37	97	515	507
Malta	26.0	7.0	8.28	40		79.59	140		
Japan	38.1	5.2	8.08	19	7	82.17	59	529	539
Sweden	23.0	8.3	9.5	68	5	80.97	78	494	495
Hong Kong	53.3	4.6	5.92	65	6	81.96	141	555	549
Iceland	28.0	8.6	9.65	47		80.79	60	507	496
New Zealand	36.2	6.5	9.26			80.48	203	519	532
Luxembourg	26.0	5.5	8.88	45		79.48	139	489	484
United Kingdom	34.0	7.9	8.16		9	79.92	206	492	514
Ireland	30.7	8.6	8.79	49	7	80.07	99	487	508
Singapore	48.1	2.3	5.89	19	2	82.06	273	562	542
Cyprus	29.0	6.0	7.29	45	10	77.66	105		
South Korea	31.4	3.7	8.11	28	16	78.81	98	546	538
Italy	32.0	8.4	7.83	39	15	80.33	113	483	489
France	32.7	9.5	7.77	35	9	81.09	96	497	498
Czech Republic	26.0	9.3	8.19	39		77.01	211	493	500
Slovenia	28.4	10.6	7.69	27	11	77.12	67	501	512
Taiwan		5.2	7.52	22		78.15	282		
Slovakia	26.0	12.5	7.35	21		75.62	185	497	490
Israel	39.2	6.4	7.48	62	15	80.86	325	447	455
Spain	32.0	20.0	8.16	36	14	81.07	159	483	488
Greece	33.0	12.0	7.92	31	9	79.8	102	466	470
Portugal	38.5	10.7	8.02	22	10	78.38	110	487	493
United States	45.0	9.0	8.18	57	16	78.24	743	487	502

Sources: The CIA's *The World Factbook,* U.S. unemployment rate from the Bureau of Labor Statistics, the Economist Intelligence Unit's *Democracy Index 2010,* Gallup, UNICEF, King's College London's World Prison Brief, Organization for Economic Cooperation and Development's Program for International Student Assessment.

if you're officially looking for work. Many people have taken part-time jobs who want full-time work. They're not counted. And in addition to the 9 percent unemployed there are about 6 percent of our people in their working years who are not counted in the unemployment numbers because they are discouraged and not "officially" looking for work, suggesting the real unemployment rate is 15 percent or higher. Overall participation in the work force by the adult population has dropped from an all-time high in 2000.

On food insecurity, measuring the percentage of people who didn't have enough money at some time in the last year to buy food, only twenty countries reported. The United States tied with South Korea for the highest percentage in need at 16 percent.

Our highest positive ranking on this list is eleventh, on Gallup's Global Wellbeing Index, which measures the percentage of people thriving in the United States at 57 percent, well below Denmark's top ranking at 82 percent.

On comparative tests, U.S. students ranked sixteenth in science, twenty-second in math. Our high school graduation rate is eighteenth, as the next chart shows. Our problems in kindergarten through twelfth-grade education are well known. In elementary school, our kids match up well with others. By the eighth grade, there's a pretty wide gap between our students and those in the highest-scoring countries. By the eleventh grade, the gap has grown into

High school graduation rates

1.	Germany	99.5%	14.	Slovakia	84.7%
2.	Finland	96.8%	15.	Hungary	84.3%
3.	Greece	96.2%	16.	Poland	83.7%
4.	Japan	93%	17.	Canada	78.9%
5.	Norway	91.9%	18.	**United States**	77.5%
6.	South Korea	91.3%	19.	Luxembourg	74.6%
7.	Ireland	89.6%	20.	New Zealand	74.5%
8.	Switzerland	89.1%	21.	Spain	74.3%
9.	United Kingdom	88.7%	22.	Sweden	74.1%
10.	Czech Republic	88%	23.	Portugal	65.1%
11.	Iceland	85.9%	24.	Turkey	58.4%
12.	Denmark	85.4%	25.	Mexico	42.6%
13.	Italy	84.9%			

No data is provided for: Australia, Austria, Belgium, Brazil, France, Netherlands, and the Russian Federation

Source: Education at a Glance 2010: OECD Indicators, www.oecd.org/edu/eag2010

a chasm. Though our best students continue to do reasonably well compared with other nations' best students, we also have a higher percentage of low-performing students than they do.*†

An even more troubling development for our long-term economic health is the trend that can be seen in the next chart. It shows our ranking, compared with other wealthy countries, in college-graduation rates. In 1995, the United States still led the world. By 2009, while we ranked third in 55- to 64-year-olds with college degrees, we ranked sixteenth in 25- to 34-year-olds with them. This shift happened because other countries improved their graduation rates over the last decade and we didn't. America is still at or near first in the world in the percentage of

*See http://www.all4ed.org/files/Facts_For_Education_Adv_ Jan 2009.pdf.

†One of the most interesting findings of the international student assessments is how well Finland is doing. Though it's a small country, its students are a diverse lot. Forty-five languages are spoken in Helsinki schools. In the 1990s, Finland's schools weren't doing well. Instead of adopting a national testing program, Finland focused on defining excellence in teaching and learning. Every teacher has a master's degree. Only one in ten applicants gets a teaching job. It's the most respected, though not the highest-paid, profession. Though they don't give any domestic tests, students do well on international tests. Only 4 percent of the schools are underperforming, and the country is rated among the very best in innovation and creativity, important twenty-first-century skills. In the United States, the approach most like Finland's is that embraced by the KIPP charter schools. They have also defined excellence in teaching and learning. Based on their test scores and the fact that their poor minority students succeed in college at a higher rate than white students, it works here too.

our young people who start college, but our dropout rate is higher, probably because of a decade in which incomes were flat or declining and the cost of college increased 75 percent.

I hope the Obama administration's student-loan program will correct much of this trend. Under the new system, the federal government will lend the money directly to students, instead of guaranteeing bank loans. That will lower student-loan costs. The students also don't need to be afraid of running up debt to get a degree, because their loans can be paid off over twenty years as a small, fixed percentage of income. That means once the program is fully implemented, no one will ever have to drop out of college again because of the cost. The new program will cost the government **$60 billion less** than the old system over a decade, $40 billion of which will go to increase Pell Grants and other student aid and work programs, with the remaining $20 billion used to reduce the debt.

If you're skeptical that this system will save money, don't be. During my administration, the Education Department gave colleges the option of using this system. It saved students $9 billion, an average of $1,300 in repayment costs on every $10,000 borrowed, and saved the taxpayers $4 billion, because once the students were able to repay their loans, almost no one defaulted.

The college graduation rate is really important, because even though many new graduates are strug-

Percentage of population that has attained higher education, by age group (2009)

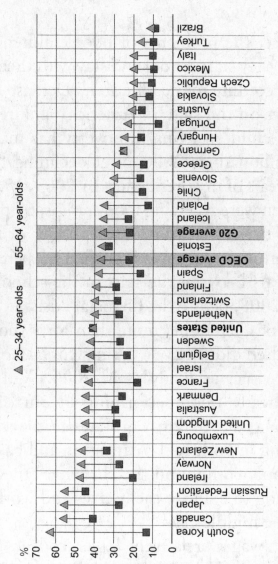

▲ 25–34 year-olds   ■ 55–64 year-olds

Countries (top to bottom): Brazil, Turkey, Italy, Mexico, Czech Republic, Slovakia, Austria, Portugal, Hungary, Germany, Greece, Slovenia, Chile, Poland, Iceland, **G20 average**, Estonia, **OECD average**, Spain, Finland, Switzerland, Netherlands, **United States**, Sweden, Belgium, Israel, France, Denmark, Australia, United Kingdom, Luxembourg, New Zealand, Norway, Ireland, Russian Federation¹, Japan, Canada, South Korea

% axis: 70, 60, 50, 40, 30, 20, 10, 0

1. Year of reference 2002.

Countries are ranked in descending order of the percentage of 25- to 34-year-olds who have attained higher education.

Source: OECD. Table A1.3a. (www.oecd.org/edu/eag2011).

Http://dx.doi.org/10.1787/888932459831.

OECD

gling to find jobs in this economy, the unemployment rate for college graduates is 4.5 percent, half the national average, and the rate for those with professional and other postgraduate degrees is around 2 percent.

Of course, the problems of poor children begin well before they start school and stay with them after they do. According to the Children's Defense Fund's 2011 report on the state of America's children, the number of children living in poverty has increased by four million since 2000, after declining for the last seven years of my presidency. By 2009, 15.6 million children were receiving food stamps, 65 percent more than ten years earlier. The number of homeless children in our schools increased 41 percent in just two years between the start of the school years 2006 and 2008, before the financial crisis. In 2010, in New York City alone, more than forty thousand schoolchildren didn't have a permanent home, more than three times as many as in 2006. With poor children already underperforming in our schools, the fact that a large majority of states are planning to cut spending in both K–12 education and basic services will only compound the challenges these kids face in trying to educate themselves and work their way into the middle class.

Stagnant wages, relatively lower college graduation rates, and limited job growth have also hurt our international rankings in an area we think of as essential to America's character: social and eco-

Change in the number of poor children in America from the previous year

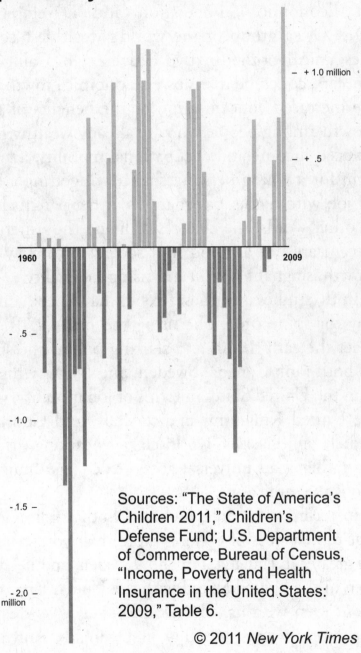

Sources: "The State of America's
Children 2011," Children's
Defense Fund; U.S. Department
of Commerce, Bureau of Census,
"Income, Poverty and Health
Insurance in the United States:
2009," Table 6.

© 2011 *New York Times*

nomic mobility. According to the latest survey, several countries have surpassed us in this category too. Two recent studies, one by the Organisation for Economic Co-operation and Development (OECD), a group of the world's wealthiest countries, and the other by two University of California scholars, conclude that slower economic growth and the increased concentration of the benefits of that growth among people who are already wealthy have reduced income and occupational mobility, a fancy term for a young person's chances of getting a better job with higher pay than his or her parents had. In other words, the chances of living the American Dream are not as good in a society with slow job growth, stagnant wages, and rising inequality.

Both studies say these trends have been under way for some time, one using the mid-1970s, the other the early 1980s as a starting point. The studies both rank Canada, Sweden, and Norway higher than the United States in terms of job mobility, with the United Kingdom, France, Italy, and Germany (which emphasizes world-class vocational training rather than universal access to college) ranking about the same as us.

In terms of income mobility, both studies agree that the chances of earning more than your parents are greater in Canada, Finland, Sweden, and Norway than in the United States, with the United Kingdom about even with us. The OECD study says there is also more income mobility in Denmark, Australia,

Germany, France, and Spain (the study was made before its recent troubles), ranking the United States tenth in an area we are accustomed to believe is a fundamental part of what it means to be an American.

It is heartening that people all over the world want to pursue their own version of the American Dream but troubling that others are doing a better job than we are of providing it to their people.

Both mobility studies conclude that the success of the nations doing better than we are is due to government policies that equalize opportunities and prepare their people to seize them.

Of course, economic mobility also depends on the availability of good jobs. In the twenty-first century, the ability of a nation to create those jobs is determined in part by the quality of its infrastructure and its information technology networks. How are we doing in those areas?

The next two charts give us an idea. The first is the World Economic Forum's assessment of the overall quality of a nation's infrastructure, including roads, bridges, railways, airports, ports, water and sewage systems, power systems, and broadband connections. On this, the United States ranks twenty-fourth out of 142 countries measured, behind all our wealthy competitors except the U.K., Australia, and Norway. Americans who have spent hours in traffic jams and at clogged airports won't be too surprised.

Americans lost $4.8 billion in earnings and 3.9 billion gallons in wasted gas while stranded in traffic last

World economic forum quality of overall infrastructure (2011)

Rank	Country	IQS*	Rank	Country	IQS*
1.	Switzerland	6.7	21.	Barbados	5.8
2.	Singapore	6.6	22.	Spain	5.8
3.	France	6.5	23.	Malaysia	5.7
4.	Hong Kong SAR	6.5	24.	**United States**	5.7
5.	Denmark	6.4	25.	Taiwan, China	5.6
6.	Finland	6.4	26.	Qatar	5.6
7.	Iceland	6.4	27.	Saudi Arabia	5.6
8.	Austria	6.3	28.	United Kingdom	5.6
9.	United Arab Emirates	6.3	29.	Czech Republic	5.6
10.	Germany	6.2	30.	Cyprus	5.5
11.	Sweden	6.1	31.	Estonia	5.5
12.	Portugal	6.1	32.	Chile	5.5
13.	Japan	6.0	33.	Slovenia	5.3
14.	Netherlands	6.0	34.	Turkey	5.3
15.	Canada	6.0	35.	Namibia	5.3
16.	Luxembourg	5.9	36.	Croatia	5.2
17.	Belgium	5.9	37.	Australia	5.2
18.	South Korea	5.9	38.	Israel	5.1
19.	Bahrain	5.9	39.	Puerto Rico	5.1
20.	Oman	5.9	40.	Lithuania	5.1

*Infrastructure Quality Score (out of 7)
Source: World Economic Forum, Executive Opinion Survey

year, according to the Texas Transportation Institute. The American Society of Civil Engineers says travel delays and substandard infrastructure (like potholes) cost Americans almost $130 billion a year. That doesn't count the economic losses of lower productivity, missed export opportunities at ports and airports, or the household costs and environmental damage created in populous areas of America where people must rely on septic tanks because there are no municipal sewage systems, or heat their homes with home heating oil rather than natural gas or electricity.

Most people also may not know that the United States spends only 1.7 percent of GDP on infrastructure, compared with 4 percent for Canada or 9 percent for China, which is trying to catch up. A big reason for this is our reluctance to raise the gas tax. That's understandable, because Americans drive a lot and their budgets are tight; buying gasoline consumes more than 10 percent of the income of many lower-income Americans. But millions of Americans pay even more in the cost of time and gas wasted in traffic jams, not to mention the costs of car repairs and lost business opportunities.

The second chart ranks nations on the quality of their broadband connections, based on the percentage of households with access, the speed of the connections, and costs. The United States ranks fifteenth out of the thirty nations studied by the Information Technology & Innovation Foundation, behind all our wealthy competitors except Germany. On the speed measure alone, we rank even lower, at twenty-eighth, according to a 2009 survey by Speed Matters. As every American knows, if only the percentage of cell phone calls interrupted by loss of the connection were measured, we'd rank even lower.

What most Americans don't know is that the average download speed of number-one-ranked **South Korea's broadband connections is four times faster**

Information Technology & Innovation Foundation (ITIF) Broadband Rankings (2008)

1. South Korea	11. Canada	21. Italy
2. Japan	12. Australia	22. Austria
3. Finland	13. United Kingdom	23. Ireland
4. Netherlands	14. Luxembourg	24. Greece
5. France	**15. United States**	25. Hungary
6. Sweden	16. Germany	26. Poland
7. Denmark	17. Belgium	27. Czech Republic
8. Iceland	18. Portugal	28. Slovakia
9. Norway	19. New Zealand	29. Turkey
10. Switzerland	20. Spain	30. Mexico

Based on household penetration, speed, and cost

than ours, because the Korean government made rapid, efficient broadband a priority. The stimulus bill provided $7.2 billion to bring high-speed Internet connections to rural areas. It will help, but it will cost more than that to move the United States into the top rank of nations. Does it matter?

It matters a lot, because speed determines the possibilities for using the Internet to create jobs and maximize innovations in telemedicine, education, energy conservation, user-friendly government services, and other areas.

WELL, ENOUGH OF THE BAD NEWS. Let's look at America's strengths. America still has by far the world's largest economy. Our per capita income is still high. According to the World Bank, it ranks sixth among the world's larger economies, tied with Finland and behind Norway, Switzerland, Denmark, Sweden, and the Netherlands. The CIA's **World Factbook,** which measures GDP per capita, ranks the United States higher, behind only Norway and Singapore. So, in spite of our high degree of income inequality, we're still doing pretty well. On overall competitiveness, the latest World Economic Forum report ranks the United States fifth, highest of any large economy, behind Switzerland, Singapore, Sweden, and Finland, just ahead of Germany, followed by the Netherlands and Denmark.

Thanks in large measure to our openness to immigrants, we're still a relatively young country. The median age of our already wealthy competitors is higher than ours, so in the future, if we can restore economic growth and slow down the rise in health-care costs, we should have a better ratio of workers to retirees and more opportunities to create more broadly shared prosperity.

America is also still the world's most entrepreneurial country. It's easy to start a small business, and for several years small businesses have accounted for a majority of our new job growth. Though other countries are working hard to catch up and surpass us, the United States is still the world's hotbed of innovation, with active research centers in university, government, and private labs and a vigorous group of venture capitalists to help early survivors grow.

We're still the world's largest exporter of goods, services, and remittances, though China and Germany have surpassed us in the export of merchandise, and trade is a smaller percentage of our national income than that of several of our competitors.

American workers are highly productive and willing to put in long hours. We have untapped natural assets, especially in natural gas and in clean energy, where we rank first or second in studies measuring nations' capacity to generate electricity from the sun and wind. And we have people here from all over the world, increasing our chances of selling products and services in fast-growing countries.

There are even large successful countries with a higher debt load than ours, led by Japan, with a national debt of more than 200 percent of its GDP, a rapidly aging population, and higher barriers to immigrants entering its workforce. The Japanese have weathered a long dry spell following their real-estate collapse in the 1990s because they have a personal savings rate of more than 20 percent of disposable income and a national passion to cut costs through greater efficiency in energy use and other areas.

The troubling thing about all these rankings and several others I haven't bothered you with is **not what they say about where we are but what they reveal about where we're going.** We simply are not doing what we have to do to stay ahead of the competition for good jobs, new businesses, and breakthrough innovations. Lots of other countries are hot on our heels with rising incomes, declining inequality, increased educational attainment, and big investments in the key drivers of today's and tomorrow's economy.

Oh, I almost forgot one critical comparison, perhaps the most important one, given our raging debate over the role of government and whether taxes are always bad. If the antigovernment activists are right, the countries catching up to or surpassing the United States in all the areas discussed in this chapter must have done it by cutting taxes, spending, and regulations—there's no other way. So here's the last chart, I promise. The numbers are the percentage of national income paid in taxes by different nations, including, for the United States, federal, state, and local taxes. Of the thirty-three nations in the OECD, we rank thirty-first in the percentage of GDP directed to taxes, with only Mexico and Chile taking a smaller percentage, and we're twenty-fifth in the percentage of GDP devoted to government spending.

There are only three ways to view this. First, the obvious conclusion: low levels of taxation and weak government investments don't necessarily bring prosperity, equal opportunity, and growth and, if too low, can prevent a nation from reaching its full potential in employment, rising incomes, and social mobility. Second, the "I don't care, I still don't like it" conclusion: even if it would be good for the country and our children's future, we just don't want the

Total tax revenue as percentage of GDP

	1965	1975	1985	1995	2000	2007	2008	2009 provisional
Australia	20.5	25.2	27.6	28.0	30.3	29.5	27.1	n.a.
Austria[1]	33.9	36.6	40.8	41.4	43.2	42.1	42.7	42.8
Belgium	31.1	39.5	44.3	43.5	44.7	43.8	44.2	43.2
Canada	25.7	32.0	32.5	35.6	35.6	33.0	32.3	31.1
Chile				19.0	19.4	24.0	22.5	18.2[4]
Czech Republic				37.6	35.3	37.3	36.0	34.8
Denmark [1]	30.0	38.4	46.1	48.8	49.4	49.0	48.2	48.2
Finland	30.4	36.6	39.8	45.7	47.2	43.0	43.1	43.1
France [1]	34.1	35.4	42.8	42.9	44.4	43.5	43.2	41.9
Germany [2]	31.6	34.3	36.1	37.2	37.2	36.0	37.0	37.0
Greece	17.8	19.4	25.5	28.9	34.0	32.3	32.6	29.4
Hungary				41.3	38.5	39.7	40.2	39.1
Iceland	26.2	30.0	28.2	31.2	37.2	40.6	36.8	34.1
Ireland	24.9	28.8	34.7	32.5	31.3	30.9	28.8	27.8
Israel [3]				37.0	36.8	36.3	33.8	31.4
Italy	25.5	25.4	33.6	40.1	42.2	43.4	43.3	43.5
Japan	18.2	20.8	27.1	26.8	27.0	28.3	28.1	n.a.
Luxembourg	27.7	32.8	39.4	37.1	39.1	35.7	35.5	37.5
Mexico			15.5	15.2	16.9	17.9	21.0	17.5[5]
Netherlands	32.8	40.7	42.4	41.5	39.6	38.7	39.1	n.a.
New Zealand	24.1	28.7	31.3	36.2	33.2	35.1	33.7	31.0
Norway	29.6	39.2	42.6	40.9	42.6	43.8	42.6	41.0
Poland				36.2	32.8	34.8	34.3	n.a.
Portugal	15.9	19.1	24.5	30.9	32.8	35.2	35.2	n.a.
Slovakia					34.1	29.4	29.3	29.3
Slovenia				39.2	37.5	37.8	37.2	37.9
South Korea		14.9	16.1	20.0	22.6	26.5	26.5	25.6
Spain [1]	14.7	18.4	27.6	32.1	34.2	37.3	33.3	30.7
Sweden	33.4	41.3	47.4	47.5	51.4	47.4	46.3	46.4
Switzerland	17.5	23.9	25.5	27.7	30.0	28.9	29.1	30.3
Turkey	10.6	11.9	11.5	16.8	24.2	24.1	24.2	24.6
United Kingdom	30.4	34.9	37.0	34.0	36.4	36.2	35.7	34.3
United States	24.7	25.6	25.6	27.8	29.5	27.9	26.1	24.0

Unweighted average:

	1965	1975	1985	1995	2000	2007	2008	
OECD Total	25.5	29.4	32.5	34.4	35.5	35.4	34.8	n.a.

n.a. indicates not available.

1. The total tax revenues have been reduced by the amount of any capital transfer that represents uncollected taxes.

2. Unified Germany beginning in 1991.

3. The data for Israel are supplied by and under the responsibility of the relevant Israeli authorities. The use of such data by the OECD is without prejudice to the status of the Golan Heights, East Jerusalem, and Israeli settlements in the West Bank under the terms of international law.

4. Secretariat estimate, including expected revenues in the 4100, 4300, 5120, and 5200 categories.

5. Secretariat estimate, including expected revenues collected by state and local governments.

OECD Tax Revenue Statistics

government to make these investments, especially with our money. Third, the ideological conclusion: all taxes are bad, all programs are a waste of money, and all regulations distort the perfect working of the free market. Therefore all charts in this chapter are wrong! Or, as my daughter and her friends used to say when they were younger, "Denial is not just a river in Egypt."

If there are any militant antitax folks still reading this book, I can hear the counterattack forming in your minds: "Clinton wants European-style social democracy! He wants to tax us to death! He's for too much government! He doesn't believe in American exceptionalism! He doesn't even love America anymore, or he wouldn't be telling us all this bad stuff!"

That's all nonsense. When I was governor of Arkansas, I raised taxes to fund education but supported tax cuts as incentives to get new jobs, eliminated the state income tax on 25 percent of our taxpayers (the bottom 25 percent), and kept our overall tax burden the second lowest in the country, just where it was when I took office. In the 1980s, Arkansas was one of the few states to gain manufacturing jobs and led our region in overall employment growth. By 1992, as I was running for president, Arkansas ranked first or second nationally in job growth all year long. When I left office as president, America's overall tax burden was less than 20 percent of GDP, about our post–World War II average, and our federal spending was a little above 18 percent of GDP, both well below most other wealthy nations.

I do believe in American exceptionalism. My life has been graced by it. I just want it to be more than a hot-button campaign slogan. That's why I want us to face facts, warts and all, and work together to give future generations the America they deserve.

Right now, in this fragile economy, I don't favor raising taxes or reducing any government spending that can create or save jobs. But as the economy recovers, I want America to embrace a balanced approach that creates jobs, raises incomes across the board, and deals with our long-term investment and debt challenges.

The most important lesson you can take from this chapter is that in the twenty-first century, the American Dream requires progress we won't achieve without effective government policies, including direct investments, incentives to speed business and job growth, and public-private partnerships to create an environment where these things can happen. Like it or not, there are a lot of things we have to do together. What are they, and what role should government play?

Part II

What We Can Do

CHAPTER 6

How Do We Get Back
in the Future Business?

First, we need to get our game face on. Critics have been betting on America's demise for more than two hundred years now. They derided George Washington's military acumen, describing him as little more than a mediocre land surveyor. As Lincoln was about to become president, an Illinois newspaper editorial called him a "baboon" who would destroy the country. Nikita Khrushchev said the Soviet Union would bury us. In the 1980s, the Japanese were going to out-produce and out-trade us into oblivion. I could go on and on. You get the picture. **No one can take the future away from us. But we can take it away from ourselves.**

Not long before the United States entered World War II, Winston Churchill famously said that America always does the right thing, "after exhaust-

ing all other alternatives." We can't afford to waste
any more time exhausting dead-end alternatives. It's
time to do the right thing. The right thing is to put
America back in the future business.

As you saw from the previous chapter comparing
America's current standing in many areas with those
of our competitors, the most successful countries
have both vigorous market economies and active,
effective governments working together to achieve
common goals.

**There is simply no evidence that we can succeed
in the twenty-first century with an antigovernment
strategy.** To get more economic growth that is more
broadly shared, we'll have to pursue the strategy that
works.

It shouldn't be all that hard. After all, America
developed it in the first place. From Theodore Roosevelt through FDR, government helped us shave the
rough edges off the Industrial Revolution, stabilize
the financial system, sustain older Americans, build
great infrastructure, bring electricity and telephone
service to rural America, mobilize to defeat the
Depression, and win World War II. And the economy kept growing. After World War II, until 1981,
government policies helped us build the world's
greatest middle class; reduce discrimination based
on race, gender, and sexual orientation; lower poverty rates; open wide the doors of college; increase
access to health care; and clean up our environment
in a way that promoted, not undermined, economic

growth. Through it all, the economy got stronger, and the competitive market created more wealth, more jobs, and rising incomes that lifted the middle class and reduced poverty.

Then we began to organize our politics around the idea that government is the problem, except for the eight years I served and President Obama's first two years. In 1994 and 2010, the voters—including those who stayed home—gave Congress to a **more radical, not conservative,** brand of antigovernment activists. I was convinced then and remain convinced today that most Americans didn't intend to take such a drastic turn in either election. They just thought they were getting too much government from the Democrats and wanted more balance. That became clear during my yearlong budget fight with Newt Gingrich and the Republicans throughout 1995. After the American people sided with my position, things settled down, and we began to work together.

How it develops this time remains to be seen. President Obama has a tough hand to play. Since the Democrats failed to raise the debt ceiling when they had the chance, in November and December 2010, his decision not to fight the Tea Party Congress and risk defeat in trying to get a bigger debt reduction deal with both spending cuts and tax hikes is understandable, though the agreement to raise the debt ceiling doesn't create more jobs now or do much to solve the long-term debt problem. In early September 2011, President Obama outlined specific plans to create more jobs, including many ideas previously advocated by both Republicans and Democrats, and to reduce the debt by $3 trillion when the economy begins to grow again.

I think that's the right thing to do, because the Tea Party bloc and their allies in Congress are convinced that you, the American voters, will reward them for continuing to be against everything. They're even against the payroll tax cuts for employers and employees that President Obama has proposed to spur hiring. It's not complicated. Saying NO keeps their contributors and base voters happy and keeps the economy weak, which advances what the Senate Republican leader, Mitch McConnell, says is their number-one priority: defeating the president in 2012. They're convinced that you'll punish him for what they do, or don't do, to keep unemployment high, wages low, and poverty rising. If they're right, they get the White House and Congress and the chance to finish what they started thirty years ago.

Of course, it doesn't have to be that way. If the fever breaks over the next few months, Republicans and Democrats could decide, as they did in 1996, to work together on our big challenges and let the American people decide in 2012 which parties and candidates have the best ideas for the future.

Meanwhile, we need to put a lot of people to work now. I think we should start with a three-part strategy: (1) put as much of the $4 trillion now held in banks and corporate treasuries back into the economy as fast as we can; (2) concentrate on the areas most likely to produce good jobs that have a positive ripple effect, jobs in modern infrastructure building, high-end manufacturing, green technologies, and exported goods and services; and (3) do literally dozens of other things that, when combined, can make a real impact now and also increase our long-term economic growth.

In early September 2011, the president outlined the proposals in his American Jobs Act. It contains about $250 billion in payroll tax cuts and hiring tax credits, and $200 billion in spending to employ construction workers in modernizing schools, rehabilitating buildings, and upgrading roads, railways, and bridges; to prevent layoffs of teachers, police officers, and firefighters; and to improve unemployment and training programs. If passed, it will give the economy a needed boost. Independent economists, including Mark Zandi, chief economist of Moody's Analytics and an adviser to Senator John McCain's 2008 presidential campaign, say the American Jobs Act will increase GDP between 1.3 and 2 percent in 2012 and create one to two million jobs.

To do better than that, we'll need more private-sector activity.

First, we have to get money flowing. Recessions created by financial crashes usually take much longer to get over, five to ten years or more, than business-cycle recessions, because banks are reluctant to lend, businesses are reluctant to borrow, corporations are reluctant to hire, and consumers are reluctant to spend. The good news is that, like Willie Sutton, we know where the money is in our distressed economy. And there's lots of it. Banks have more than $2 trillion in cash reserves uncommitted to loans. And businesses of all sizes have about that much uncommitted to investment. Just three big banks, Citigroup, JPMorgan Chase, and Wells Fargo, have in total more than $1 trillion in cash. The top twenty nonbank corporations, companies like GE, Microsoft, Google, Apple, Johnson & Johnson, Coca-Cola, ExxonMobil, Walmart, and Procter & Gamble, have about $350 billion.

Since banks can lend, conservatively, $10 for every dollar they hold in reserves, U.S. banks have the capacity, in theory, to end the entire global recession. Companies could invest their cash in new products that would increase hiring today or in research and development that would increase employment today and even more in the future. Unfortunately, banks are reluctant to lend, and loan demand is weak. As for the big companies, many executives have decided, at least for now, not to invest in future growth but to buy back their stock instead, increasing earnings per share and, in the process, earning bigger bonuses for top management, once again widening the gap between themselves and their own employees and doing nothing to put America back to work.

The rest of this chapter presents a set of proposals to increase bank lending and corporate investment, to create more jobs that pay well, and to make sure we have enough people trained to fill them. Several of these proposals are included in the president's American Jobs Act, which contains other good ideas as well. Right now, the United States needs all the good ideas we can get. If you disagree with any of these proposals, or if you've got a better idea, I invite you to share your ideas on social media platforms using the hashtag #backtowork.

Now, BACK TO BUSINESS. WHAT CAN we do to unlock the money?

1. **End the mortgage mess as quickly as possible.** Even though banks have off-loaded most of their mortgages to Fannie Mae and Freddie Mac, they still hold some nonperforming ones, under $200 billion worth, for which they have to keep cash in reserve. They've still got plenty of unencumbered cash reserves, but they remain reluctant to lend, because the continuing mortgage failures are glutting the market with empty houses, keeping the housing market depressed, and holding down the entire economy. Seventy-five percent of household debt, still high at more than 110 percent of disposable income, is mortgage debt, with more than 25 percent of American homes now worth less than their mortgages.

The debt overhang of financial crashes is the main reason they normally take five years or more to get over, rather than the one-year or shorter recovery period for the typical recession. Large lingering debt is a big reason the stimulus program kept us from falling into a full depression but couldn't lift us into a full recovery.

A rapid, comprehensive effort to resolve the ongoing mortgage crisis would have four benefits. It would clean up bank balance sheets, freeing them up to lend; reduce the severe economic stress on millions of consumers, allowing more of their incomes to be spent for normal consumption; turn empty houses now depressing the market into properly maintained rental properties; and create a lot of jobs in preparing already foreclosed-on houses to be rented out.

To do that, we need a program that is simple and more accessible than the administration's current modification program, HAMP. It has helped a lot of people, almost one million, but not enough. The initiative to encourage mortgage write-downs to the value of the home has helped far fewer. Ideally, the program would have these components:

a) Every delinquent homeowner whose mortgage is worth more than the house should have the mortgage principal written down or its term extended at a low interest rate, if doing so would enable the homeowner to make the smaller payments. If over the life of the mortgage or at an earlier sale the value of the home goes up again and it is sold at a profit, the owner should share the profit with the lender. Ocwen Loan Servicing, based in Atlanta, is already offering shared appreciation plans.

b) The borrowers who can't make even the reduced payments should be given the option of swapping their deed for a multiyear lease, with modest rental payments sufficient to cover taxes, insurance, and maintenance, and the option to buy the home back at market value when the lease expires, or earlier, if the borrower's financial circumstances permit. Congress has been debating this option since 2008. It should be done now. And it won't add to the budget deficit.

Harvard University economist Kenneth Rogoff has suggested a variation on this approach. Rather than have the homeowner become a renter, Rogoff recommends letting the bank convert a portion of the mortgage into an equity investment, thus reducing the homeowner's monthly payments to an affordable level without reducing the obligation of the homeowner to pay off the debt by reconverting the bank's ownership interest back into mortgage payments when circumstances improve. As governor of Arkansas, I proposed and the Arkansas legislature passed a mechanism similar to Rogoff's for state-chartered bank loans to troubled farmers. The state banks didn't want to foreclose on farmers but didn't want bank regulators to cite them for holding too much bad debt. Our bill allowed them to convert the debt into partial ownership of the farms. A farmer who avoided foreclosure had the right to turn the bank's equity position back into debt as soon as he could make the payments. Rogoff's idea could work.

c) If neither option works for the homeowner, then foreclosure should be expedited, coupled with assistance in finding an affordable rental option.

d) Meanwhile, the government should incentivize banks, as holders and servicers of mortgages, along with Fannie Mae, Freddie Mac, the VA, and the Federal Housing Administration (FHA), to get their housing stock into rentable shape and to charge the lowest possible rates so that the houses can be filled more quickly and don't deteriorate further. This is much better than allowing Fannie and Freddie to continue to dump thousands of foreclosed-on houses onto the market each month, further depressing housing prices and the value of occupied homes.

e) If we want to create even more jobs with this effort, the houses to be rented should be given energy audits and retrofits. Typically, utility savings of 20 percent or more can be achieved with just one day of retrofit work by knowledgeable contractors. Though the utility bills will go down, the renters would continue to pay the same rent until the cost of the retrofit is paid off, usually in twelve to eighteen months. Then the rent payment would be reduced to reflect the 20 percent reduction in the utility bill. Meanwhile, every $1 billion spent on home retrofits creates about eight thousand jobs. The banks could finance the retrofits at little or no risk because bonded contractors will guarantee the savings to get the work. Or the Treasury Department could finance them with money from the unspent TARP funds allocated to the mortgage problem. I believe the total is more than $40 billion. Like the banks, the government would get the money back plus interest.

So why aren't we doing this already? A number of news articles I've read recently suggest that banks are reluctant to write down mortgages because they make more money on foreclosures. The bankers I've talked to about this say it isn't so, because the costs of maintaining foreclosed property are greater than the foreclosure fees.

It seems to me there are three obstacles to rapid, comprehensive resolution of the problem.

First, the public entities that hold mortgages, the VA and the FHA, often don't allow principal reduction, even when doing so would have a positive economic impact. The publicly created big mortgage holders, Fannie Mae and Freddie Mac, don't either, even though they received more than $140 billion from the government to help them survive after they made large purchases of subprime mortgages from

2004 through 2007. One recent news article, based on Fannie Mae's own records, claims Fannie spent $27,000 to foreclose on one home with a delinquency of only $3,000.

Why are they doing this?

When Freddie and Fannie got their bailouts, Congress put them under the supervision of the Federal Housing Finance Agency. Its interim director, Edward DeMarco, says his mission is to conserve Fannie's and Freddie's assets, not to restore the health of the housing market. Given a narrow interpretation of his legislative mandate, he may be right. He's been defended by Sheila Bair, former director of the Federal Deposit Insurance Corporation, who did more than any other Bush administration official to warn of, and try to fend off, the crash, and has made constructive proposals to fix it. Still, the problem with DeMarco's position is that in opposing writing down mortgages or refinancing them at lower interest rates, he may save Fannie Mae and Freddie Mac money today, but not in the long run, because until we resolve the underlying problem the value of housing stock will continue to decrease, making even more mortgages valued higher than homes. Something has to be done to change this.

Fannie Mae, Freddie Mac, the VA, and the FHA shouldn't be blocking mortgage modifications or pushing for foreclosures on modest delinquencies. According to Bank of America, of the millions of delinquent mortgages it services, 60 percent are held by Fannie Mae and Freddie Mac, 20 percent by the VA and the FHA. They have to be on board to make this work.

The second problem is that there's no single authority with the power to institute and accelerate this process. The states' attorneys general are trying to reach a comprehensive settlement over the mistakes made by mortgage issuers. Even if they do, the foreclosure process is different from state to state. If a delinquent homeowner decides to fight foreclosure with every available option, the process can take from two to eight years. And as yet, the bankers that service the mortgages and the entities that own them haven't reached agreement on clear standards for mortgage modifications or workable foreclosures.

The U.S. Treasury Department is trying to broker a comprehensive settlement covering all the states and all the mortgage servicers and owners. In the Bank of America case, the investors who sued the bank to recover their investments in overvalued mortgages agreed, in return for $8.5 billion in compensation from Bank of America, to allow a court to resolve all the questions regarding individual cases in a transparent process. Any settlement involving the states, the mortgage owners, and the servicers needs to have a similar effective, open, and timely process to resolve these questions. Prolonged delays might help some homeowners, but they won't eliminate the serious drag of all the debt on the entire economy soon enough.

The third problem is that many Americans who didn't take out risky mortgages and are making their payments every month don't think it's fair to modify the mortgages of people who shouldn't have taken them out in the first place and should face the consequences of their mistakes.

That's a defensible position that in normal times should govern our policy. But it shouldn't control our actions today. Why? Because the housing market collapse has hurt the entire economy so much that a lot of people who can't make mortgage payments today were reasonable in thinking they'd never default when they signed the mortgage papers. Because every foreclosure punishes more people than the imprudent borrower, it drives down the prices of all the houses in the neighborhood. And because now so many homes have been foreclosed on, or are about to be, the total impact has depressed overall housing values, shrinking the biggest source of family wealth for millions of innocent bystanders. The over 25 percent of mortgages now worth more than their homes' value include many on which payments are not delinquent. And if they're written down on terms that require the owner to share future profits with the lender if the house rises in value, the so-called moral hazard argument has much less force.

We can't put people back to work in an economy where consumers spend less, banks don't lend, businesses don't borrow, state and local governments reduce employment and support for schools, and the federal government is cutting back too. The mortgage problem is freezing us in place.

Under these circumstances, opposing mortgage modifications because some people don't deserve them is cutting off our nose to spite our face. It reminds me of the old Cajun story of Ramon, who liked to carry expensive cigars in the front pocket of his coat. One day his friend Pierre noticed that he had replaced the cigars with sticks of dynamite. When he asked why, Ramon replied, "You know that no-good Jacques? Every time I see him, he says hello, then slaps me in the chest and destroys my good cigars. I'll show him." Pierre said, "But, Ramon, if the dynamite explodes, it'll kill you." Ramon said, "I know that, but I'll blow his damn hand off too!" Requiring all delinquent homeowners to face the full consequences of their mortgages is a luxury we can't afford. All the rest of us are getting hurt too.

While all the ideas that follow will create jobs and increase growth, it's going to be very hard to return to full employment and rising incomes unless we reduce the debt overhang of the mortgage crisis. We need to clear it up as soon as possible.

2. **Let people with government-guaranteed mortgages who aren't delinquent refinance their mortgages at the current low interest rate.** This step would help the economy with a multiyear stimulus that doesn't cost the taxpayers anything. Home

mortgage rates are now down to 4 percent. Fewer than one million people have taken advantage of the government's Home Affordable Refinance Program (HARP). But there are more than twenty-two million homeowners who are current on government-backed mortgages with an average valuation of $150,000 and an average interest rate of 5.6 percent. There is widespread criticism that refinancing fees for the loans backed by Fannie Mae and Freddie Mac are excessive, especially for borrowers without perfect credit ratings. In some cases the fees may be so significant that they essentially eliminate the benefits. The assumption is that government servicers have instituted the fees because they are against refinancing, which would hurt their cash flow. Professor Glenn Hubbard and his colleagues have suggested creating a simplified process, applying a flat $4/10$ of 1 percent fee for refinancing any fully performing loan that Fannie or Freddie guarantees. The flat fee is higher than such fees have been historically but less than they are charging currently, and still provides some compensation for the lower income the new loans will generate.

If even half of the twenty-two-plus million homes were refinanced at 4 percent, the average family's mortgage payment would drop $2,500 a year, putting close to $30 billion a year into the pockets of middle-class families, reducing the rates of foreclosure, and substantially increasing the money families can spend to help get the economy going again.

This is a benefit millions of responsible Americans could receive that would help us all. On the other hand, without refinancing, if even one million of the homeowners default—less than 5 percent—the foreclosure costs would be about $90 billion. Shutting them out of the current lower interest rates just doesn't make sense.

3. **The Federal Reserve should give the banks an incentive to lend.** Another thing that might increase bank lending is to adopt an idea that is working for Sweden. Currently, because interest rates are low and banks are reluctant to lend, they keep a lot of cash on deposit with the Federal Reserve, at no cost. When the crash occurred, Sweden's manufacturing sector took a terrible beating. Sweden was in a better position than the United States to deal with it, in part because the government had a large budget surplus of 3.6 percent of GDP. However, like their U.S. counterparts, Swedish banks had plenty of capital but were reluctant to lend and so deposited a lot of the money with the central bank. To encourage bank lending, the central bank began charging Swedish banks a small fee, a quarter of 1 percent, to hold their money. Now Sweden is growing at about 5.5 percent, much faster than the United States. One reason is the more rapid resumption of bank lending. **If the Fed imposed even a modest fee of one-fourth of 1 percent on bank deposits it holds,** the banks might be more willing to lend so they

could make, not lose, money on the cash they have. It's worth a try.

An investment banker friend suggested what might be a better way to achieve the same goal. He said many banks are doing well by collecting mortgage payments without making loans because they no longer pay interest on deposits. He believes that if the Fed required 1 percent to be paid on deposits by banks with low loan-to-deposit ratios, they'd make more loans, especially to small businesses. One of these ideas is worth a try.

4. **Give corporations incentives to bring more money back to the United States.** Beyond bank holdings, the only available large concentration of cash is in corporate treasuries. A lot of it is being held overseas. One reason corporations don't repatriate the money they make in other countries is that they have to pay U.S. taxes on the income when it comes home, reducing their earnings and giving them an incentive to reinvest it in new production and research facilities in other countries. Another reason is that other nations are more aggressive than the United States in doing what American states and cities do: providing positive incentives for companies to locate in their countries and helping companies with operations there already to expand.

In 2011, Andrew Liveris, CEO of Dow Chemical, a U.S. company with global operations that has maintained 40 percent of its workforce in America while two-thirds of its sales are in other countries, released a book titled **Make It in America.** It has several suggestions for increasing companies' investment in the United States. Some of them would require congressional action, but this is one area in which we might be able to get bipartisan agreement.

As Liveris points out, the cost of labor is not preventing good jobs in advanced manufacturing and related research and development activities from being created in America. Labor is increasingly a smaller percentage of overall costs in sophisticated manufacturing, and our labor costs are already competitive with Germany's, the world's most successful exporter of high-end manufactured products. Also, our workers are highly productive, reducing the disparity in costs with countries in which employees earn less but are also less efficient. The United States is having trouble in manufacturing because other countries are outcompeting us with lower tax rates, more tax breaks, loans, and some outright grants to offset start-up costs. Other countries' governments also often pledge to buy a new factory's products to minimize the risks of losing money in the early years. Why would countries like Germany and Singapore do this? Because they know every new high-quality manufacturing job creates on average 2.5 other jobs as long as the plant is running.

The United States doesn't do this enough. A couple of years ago, Los Angeles was trying to recruit a foreign company to build fast trains for a planned high-speed-rail network to connect California's most populous areas. Both the company and its major competitor for the federally funded project were based in Europe. The big difference was that one company planned to make all the railcars in Los Angeles, creating several thousand high-paying jobs, while the other planned to import them from its home country. Eventually, the Los Angeles proposal fell apart for other reasons, but it is relevant to this discussion. Why? Because the federal government told Los Angeles that since federal money would pay for the fast trains, the very different impacts on the local economy of the two proposals could not be considered in awarding the bid! In other words, if the performance, safety, and customer-comfort qualities of the two products were identical and the bid of the company committed to manufacture railcars in America was $100 higher than the importer's bid, the importer should win the contract paid for with your tax dollars. This is nuts.

In 1993, when I supported an increase in the corporate tax rate on income above $10 million from 34 to 36 percent to reduce the deficit, it made sense because our rates were still highly competitive with those of other countries. That's not true anymore. When companies like Intel, HP, Microsoft, and Dell opened manufacturing plants in Ireland, they did so in part because the Irish cut corporate taxes to 12.5 percent.* The average European tax rate is 23 percent.

---

*Ireland has lost a lot of its good jobs since the crash, because its banks were among the most highly leveraged in Europe. Once the Irish work through the debt overhang, they'll be highly competitive again.

Among wealthy nations, we now have the second-highest corporate tax rate in the world, and because of recent changes in other countries we're now the only wealthy nation that taxes income earned overseas when it's brought back home. We've also fallen to seventeenth in the level of our research and development tax incentives. We have to become more competitive. Big corporations don't get hurt by the current system. They just put plants in other places, create good jobs there, and leave their earnings there.

In the future, we'll have to design a progressive revenue system that relies more on personal income and consumption taxes, like the value-added tax, which also would help to increase our exports, because they escape the last step of tax, making our products more affordable in other markets.

For now, I think the Democrats and Republicans should work together to amend the corporate tax laws with the understanding that the tax rates would go down but the revenue wouldn't, by broadening the tax base through the elimination and tightening of credits and deductions as the Simpson-Bowles Commission recommended. Remember, while **our tax rate is 35 percent, our tax take is 23 percent** of corporate income, because of a wide array of credits and deductions that reduce some big corporations' tax burden to less than 20 percent of income. If the percentage of income we take is competitive, why do we need to change? Because the benefits of the credits and deductions are unevenly distributed and often go to companies that won't, or can't, create nearly as many jobs in the United States as companies that actually pay the higher rate.

While writing this book, I learned that many large U.S.–based companies publish their overall employment figures but don't break them down by country. Apparently, they're concerned about bad publicity. Andrew Liveris published Dow's numbers in his book, but he's proud of the fact that Dow has 40 percent of its employment in the United States compared with one-third of its sales here. It would be helpful to know how companies claiming large credits and deductions rank in the ratio of employment to sales in the United States. Then we could design a corporate tax reform proposal that would target more tax relief to the job creators.

I do disagree with one element of the Simpson-Bowles plan. I think we should keep the research and development incentive and increase it. It will more than pay for itself, because more and more companies want their research operations located near their factories, to get the quickest possible feedback and implementation of positive discoveries.

5. **Let companies repatriate the cash now with no tax liability if it's reinvested to create new jobs.** Even if the two parties agree to work together in good faith, it could take a year or more to reform the corporate tax laws. Meanwhile, I think we should make another effort to bring a lot of the overseas earnings of U.S. companies back home. The 2004 effort to

do this, which gave corporations a grace period to repatriate money and have it taxed at a 5.25 percent rate, was widely considered a bust, because almost none of the money was invested to create new jobs. Instead, most of it went to pay dividends, buy back stocks to raise their price, and increase executive pay. The three companies that repatriated the most cash, 20 percent of the total, actually cut thirty thousand jobs in the United States. While the government did get a onetime increase in revenues, it's estimated that the Treasury lost $80 billion over a decade on money that would have trickled back into the United States, even at the higher rate.

We now know that since all other wealthy nations have abandoned taxing the income their corporations earn in other countries, we're not going to get that $80 billion. Therefore, I think the president should offer U.S. companies a three-part deal: (1) an honest effort to work with Congress to develop a competitive corporate tax system, with lower rates that will save money for most companies while requiring those paying far below the average rate of 23 percent to pay their fair share; (2) the ability to repatriate the money now and do whatever they want with it, though at a higher rate than the 2004 tax holiday rate, say 15 or 20 percent, with the money going to seed an infrastructure bank or, if that can't be done, to fund infrastructure grants to states; and (3) the ability to repatriate with **no tax liability any funds they can prove are spent to**

increase net new jobs in the United States. We're not going to get the money in taxes anyway. Let's give companies a real incentive to put America back to work. If they just want it to increase dividends and compensation, they'll pay 15 to 20 percent to reap the personal gains, and we can use the money to repair and modernize our infrastructure.*

6. **Pass President Obama's payroll tax cuts.** In the American Jobs Act, the president has proposed a 50 percent cut in payroll taxes for 160 million workers, a tax cut worth about $1,500 to the typical family, and a 50 percent cut in employer payroll taxes on the first $5 million in payroll. If enacted by Congress, it will have a positive impact on employees who'll have more spending money and employers who believe that, with more employees, they can increase sales of their products or services. All the independent studies show that the positive impact of payroll tax cuts is considerably greater than that of keeping the Bush-era tax cuts for high-income individuals.

The president has also proposed a **complete payroll tax holiday for all net new jobs and increased**

*There's one big roadblock to this proposal. The Joint Committee on Taxation will "score" repatriation as costing $80 billion in revenues, even though we're the only OECD country still taxing overseas income. Under the budget agreement the administration would have to come up with $80 billion of further cuts to gain far less than that to seed the infrastructure bank. If this unrealistic position can't be changed, Congress must complete the corporate tax reform as soon as possible.

wages, up to $50 million in payroll increases. We don't collect payroll taxes on nonexistent jobs anyway. This would help employers of all sizes as well as their employees. There are ways to prevent abuse and to require that the tax be paid if, for example, already-employed workers are counted as new ones, so that employers will get the benefit only if they add jobs.

In addition to the large tax cuts, the president has proposed a $4,000 tax credit for employers who hire people who've been out of work for more than six months, rising to $5,600 for unemployed veterans and $9,600 for disabled veterans.

As we squeeze debt out of the economy, bring corporate money back into it, and provide payroll tax relief, there are some other things government can do that could make a big difference.

Before I get into the specifics of what and why, we should look at the nature of our jobs challenge.

Even in good times, every country needs an economic strategy designed to speed the development of business and job growth in the most promising areas. That is especially true in nations with more open trading systems, where the competition is stiff and nothing can be taken for granted. Remember what happened to job growth in the first decade of the twenty-first century before the crash in September 2008. It was virtually nonexistent, because all our growth was concentrated in housing, consumer spending, and finance. The first two were limited by the capacity of average Americans to take on more debt, especially when they weren't getting pay raises.

The financial sector, facing limited opportunities to make money the old-fashioned way, by providing issues of new equity or debt to help companies grow and hire, resorted to ever more esoteric devices to transfer mortgage risks away from those who had taken them, to hedge against possible losses, or just to gamble on whether mortgages or other assets were going to go up or down in value. There was an enormous amount of money moving around, but it didn't create employment and, in the end, wound up costing millions of jobs. The people who made a percentage on each deal did well, but because of the nature of the investments there was no trickle down. The net effect was to increase inequality, weaken once profitable businesses, and reduce employment.

We need a strategy that will create jobs and expand businesses, one that includes profitable opportunities for the financial sector to invest in broad-based growth. All of us have a big stake in putting America back to work. For one thing, we can't solve the debt problem without more growth. Without growth, tax increases won't produce the necessary revenues, and spending cuts will be outpaced by spending increases related to unemployment and poverty. It will take strong growth, spending cuts, and revenue increases to make a real dent in the annual deficit and our long-term debt problem.

In August 2011, I was at home, channel-surfing, when I saw the Dallas Mavericks owner and high-tech entrepreneur Mark Cuban appearing as a panelist on Bill Maher's show. They were discussing the relative merits of President Obama's budget approach and the Tea Party's "no new taxes" position. Cuban said he didn't mind paying more taxes but "Clinton's tax increases" had nothing to do with the move from deficits to surpluses during my administration. According to him, the tech boom did it all.

Cuban was wrong, but he wasn't all wrong. I had the good fortune to become president at the moment when the information technology (IT) revolution broke out of its strongholds in Silicon Valley, Massachusetts, Texas, and northern Virginia into virtually all American businesses and homes. During my eight years, IT jobs represented only 8 percent of total employment but accounted for more than 20 percent of job growth and more than 25 percent of income growth. So the tech boom did lead to higher-than-estimated tax revenues, which enabled the United States to get its budget in balance earlier than either my administration or the Congressional Budget Office first predicted.

But our economic plan, especially the 1993 budget, also made a big difference, for two reasons. First, the budget reversed twelve years of trickle-down economics. The combination of serious spending reductions and revenue increases drove interest rates down and sent the bond market roaring. Business investment increased, and lower annual interest costs on all loans and credit purchases saved $2,200 a year for the average family, providing more money for Americans to spend on computers and other tech products. Second, because accelerating the spread of information technology was at the heart of our economic strategy, we took a number of other steps that helped produce more jobs and growth, including the E-Rate, which saved schools, hospitals, and libraries $2 billion in Internet access costs; the decision to oppose taxing Internet sales for a few years to get e-commerce up and going; and the new telecommunications law, which fostered competition and gave many entrepreneurs the chance to hold their own with large companies.

I left office just as the so-called tech bubble was deflating, bringing in its wake a short recession. IT stocks had gone through the roof in the late 1990s, as demand for telecommunications products and services increased an astonishing 500 percent a year between 1997 and 1999. The recession was short-lived, largely because the bursting bubble dropped the growth rate to "only" 50 percent a year. Soon the American economy was growing again, but without many new jobs, because we didn't follow the 1990s IT boom with a new source of job growth for the first decade of the twenty-first century.

When he was governor of Texas, President George W. Bush signed legislation that helped make his state first in the nation in the production of electricity from wind. After he became president, his Energy Department released a study saying that with an adequate transmission system, 20 percent or more of our nation's electricity could come from the wind that blows from North Dakota's border with Canada to south Texas's border with Mexico. If clean energy had been targeted as our source of new jobs in the last decade, a lot more of them would have been created.

Even if we can get more money flowing with steps like those I outlined above, we still have to have at least one big source of new, well-paying jobs. In his first two years, President Obama identified and pushed to implement four of them: building a twenty-first-century infrastructure, leading the world in the production of green energy and energy conservation technologies, restoring America's manufacturing base, and doubling exports.

The Tea Party bloc in the House will almost certainly oppose any congressional action in these areas if it involves new spending. That's an ideological nonstarter for them, whether it would work or not. And the Senate Republicans will try to filibuster any new spending because they're afraid it will work. Nevertheless, I hope the president will propose what he thinks the country needs. Who knows what will come out of the debate? Maybe something good.

Let's look at the benefits investments in these areas could bring.

7. **Build a twenty-first-century infrastructure.** Millions of jobs could, and should, be created to maximize America's opportunities for economic growth and a better quality of life in the twenty-first century. If you look at where the world is going and how fast it's getting there, we clearly need much faster broadband connections; a smart electrical grid; more efficient ports and airports; and an upgrade of our old investments in roads, bridges, rails, and water and sewage systems. The stimulus allocated some money to begin those efforts, but not enough, and it's largely been spent. The antigovernment members of Congress and their supporters in the country say we can't afford to do these things. I think they sometimes forget that the "American exceptionalism" they embrace with words was built by visionary deeds. During the Depression, the Works Progress Administration and the Civilian Conservation Corps employed more than eight million people building projects that still benefit us today.

A good place to start is the infrastructure-bank legislation supported by the president in his jobs speech. It's co-sponsored in the Senate by John Kerry, Democrat from Massachusetts, and Kay Bailey Hutchison, Republican from Texas, and in the House by Rosa DeLauro, Democrat from Connecticut. The bill envisions building a twenty-first-century infrastructure with public-private partnerships. It could take investments from both the private sector and foreign governments flush with cash and looking for a safe place to put it. This is a good idea that has been discussed for years. Many other countries build or operate public projects with private investment. As long as there are high standards for performance and safety, we should too. Of course, the federal government has to put up some money. We could start with $10 billion or $20 billion, funded by the extra income flowing to the Treasury from the Federal Reserve's profits on the investments it made to avert a full-scale depression. Or we could kick in the revenues corporations will pay if we allow them to repatriate income earned in other countries for reasons other than job generation. In either case, ordinary Americans would see some positive benefits from the bailout money and corporate cash surpluses. And the returns on investment are huge: it's estimated that $10 billion in infrastructure investment could generate an economic gain of $600 billion over ten years.

We might be able to raise even more money by letting all Americans get in on the act. Americans are saving more, but most aren't earning money on what they hold, because interest rates are low and the stock market is volatile. I'd like to see the president seek renewed legislative authority for Build America Bonds, to be sold in amounts from $100 to $1 million. The proceeds would be deposited in the infrastructure bank, with the bonds maturing ten years after they're bought. That would put them outside the so-called budget window, and by the time they're due, the huge returns on modern infrastructure will generate more than enough revenue to pay them off.

Perhaps the Federal Reserve could also invest in the infrastructure bank or Build America Bonds to finance it. As we know, the Fed earns, even in normal times, a lot of money on its investments, mostly in Treasury issues, then turns the income over to the government. I don't know if the Fed has legal authority to invest in an infrastructure bank that would pay back the investment plus interest, but if it is legal to do so, I think it's a good idea.

8. **Speed up the process for approving and completing infrastructure projects.** The recent Japanese earthquake and tsunami did an enormous amount of damage, including tearing a hole forty feet deep in a sizable section of a large highway. The Japanese repaired it in just six days. Construction workers have been rebuilding a small bridge over a railroad track in Chappaqua, New York, where Hillary and I live, for three years. The comparison isn't quite fair, because in Japan everything was shut down and in Chappaqua a lot of work has to be done at night, so that people can use the bridge in the daytime. Still, three years is a long time. President Obama has committed to streamline the process for large infrastructure projects, and I'm confident it can be done

without compromising environmental or safety standards.

THE SUREST WAY TO CREATE JOBS, cut costs, enhance national security, cut the trade deficit by up to 50 percent, and fight global warming is to change the way we produce and consume energy. Even though the climate change deniers seem to have succeeded in making their position a core tenet of anti-government ideology, there is a case to be made on economics alone.

The main reason there has been no international agreement to cut greenhouse-gas emissions is that too many decision makers still don't believe we can do it without curbing economic growth and too many carbon emitters keep reinforcing that notion.

Lately, the opponents of green energy have started going after the economics hard, claiming green jobs cost over $1 million each and playing up the failure of a solar company that received more than $500 million in loan guarantees from the Department of Energy. The critics claim this example proves green tech is a dead end.

They're wrong. In July 2011, according to a report issued by the Brookings Institution and Battelle, newer clean-tech jobs grew 8.3 percent from 2003 to 2010, twice as fast as jobs in other occupations, and median wages were 20 percent higher than for other occupations, almost $44,000, compared with

$38,616. The sector has continued to grow through the recession and now accounts for 2.7 million jobs. Its exports in goods and services amounted to $53.9 billion in 2009.

These trends have developed in the face of a severe global recession and even though, unlike our major competitors, the United States hasn't passed legislation to limit carbon emissions through a cap-and-trade system or a carbon tax, or adopted a clear standard to increase the percentage of our electricity generated by clean energy by a fixed date, or committed to a clear long-term strategy of incentives to encourage large investments in clean energy and efficiency.

We've done as well as we have because of America's enormous capacity to generate energy from clean sources and to improve efficiency; the large number of entrepreneurs, innovators, and financiers committed to a clean-energy future; and federal investments, tax incentives, and rule making since 2007, especially in the stimulus bill, that directed the equivalent of $800 per household to clean-energy funding, loan guarantees, and tax incentives, more than $90 billion in total.

The progress in wind energy is particularly impressive. On a windy day in Texas, wind power can spike to 25 percent of total generation. It's 20 percent in Iowa. More than 50 percent of the contents of current turbines installed in the United States are made in America, with more to come. In Michigan, URV

USA is constructing the first foundry built in America in decades to provide the most up-to-date wind turbine casting. In 2009, enough new wind capacity was installed to power three million homes. And our wind power potential is staggering—37 trillion kilowatt hours, almost ten times our existing needs.

You can tell I'm a big fan of President Obama's energy policy and of the leadership of the secretary of energy, Steven Chu. But they're facing a lot of competition in the battle for clean-energy jobs. Germany and China lead the world in clean-energy exports; China has installed more wind capacity than the United States, has about half the global market in solar cells, and is racing ahead with tens of billions of dollars in new investments and incentives, in a determined effort to lead the world in both the installation and the export of clean-tech products. Other countries are moving up, too. European countries lead the world in offshore wind power generation. India is investing massive sums in solar power. Brazil generates almost 80 percent of its electricity from hydropower, burns more ethanol from sugarcane than gasoline in its cars, and hasn't even begun to seriously develop its considerable potential for wind and solar.

This is an area of enormous opportunity for us.* However, besides the need for a renewable-energy

---

*If you want more information, check out Google.org's **The Impact of Clean Energy Innovation.**

standard and other changes that the current antigovernment majority in the House of Representatives opposes, there are real challenges to creating
more jobs and starting new businesses providing
clean energy and increasing efficiency, rooted in the
lack of longer-term financing readily available for
the construction of traditional power plants and the
relative complexity of more decentralized green-tech
operations compared with big coal-fired generators.

Almost all the costs of solar and wind power, for
example, are front-loaded, while the economic benefits in lower annual costs take time to realize. And
building a new coal-fired power plant is simple. A
utility gets approval from one regulatory body, hires
one contractor to build the plant, secures a sup-
plier of the coal, and gets to bill the customers over
a twenty-year period, merging the cost of the plant
with the annual cost of the coal. The annual costs of
solar and wind are almost nothing, but the up-front
costs are high (though dropping steadily as production goes up and technology improves), without a
coal-like payback option of twenty years.

To a lesser extent, the same thing is true of energy
efficiency. To achieve this on a large scale, building
owners should be able to offset for the cost of retrofits with savings they will realize from lower utility
bills, eliminating large out-of-pocket expenses in a
down economy. Savings of 30 or 40 percent typically take six to seven years to pay off, with interest,
after which the utility bill is reduced forever. The

problem is that most Americans don't have access to this kind of "Just Say Yes" financing.

Why is this so important? Because, on average, every billion dollars invested in a new coal-fired plant yields 870 jobs. The same amount invested in solar creates 1,900; in wind, 3,300, if the turbines and blades are made in the country where they're put up; in big building retrofits, 7,000; in home retrofits, up to 8,000 jobs.

To maximize job creation and other benefits, we have to do a number of things. Let's start with conservation, the biggest bang for the buck, and a real opportunity. McKinsey & Company estimates that with an investment of $520 billion in efficiency improvements, we could save $1.2 trillion by 2020 and cut consumption 23 percent. That's a return on investment of more than two to one, plus a large number of new jobs.

9. **Launch an aggressive, fifty-state building retrofit initiative.** Recently, the Empire State Building in New York City completed a comprehensive energy overhaul, becoming the world's largest building to get a high LEED (Leadership in Energy and Environmental Design) rating from the U.S. Green Building Council. The project put 275 people to work, doing things like changing the heating and air-conditioning system; putting new, more efficient glass in the windows; and installing new lighting. The work was overseen by Johnson Controls, the

energy service company whose technology was used to maximize energy savings with temperature and lighting controls and devices that track energy use. As part of the contract, Johnson guaranteed that usage, and in utility bills, would be reduced 38 percent. That means if the savings don't materialize, Johnson has to make up the difference. Since, like all businesses, it likes to get paid for its work, the actual savings will probably be 40 percent or more. At 38 percent savings, the project will pay for itself in four and a half years, after which the Empire State's utility bills will drop dramatically.

If this is such a good deal, why isn't everyone doing it? Because all the costs are up front and few building owners, public or private, have enough cash on hand to afford them. What's the answer? Let the owners borrow the money and pay it back, plus interest, from their utility savings. That would create a more friendly "Just Say Yes" system. Why isn't it happening? Because many building owners either have too much debt to take out new loans or are not deemed creditworthy, because bankers aren't sure they'll own the building for the four to seven years it would take to pay the costs of a major retrofit from utility savings only.

There are simple ways to solve this, though they require legislative action to do nationwide. First, the government could set up a Small Business Administration–like loan guarantee program to assure the banks they will be repaid. A $15 billion fund could guarantee $150 billion in loans and create a million jobs. Remember, this is a backup guarantee that probably won't cost the taxpayers a penny, because the savings will have already been guaranteed by the contractor.

An even better way to do it would be to let the utilities finance the retrofits, since they get the extra energy capacity retrofits provide to sell to other customers. To do that, utilities have to be permitted to "decouple" their rates from energy usage, charging slightly more per kilowatt hour on retrofitted buildings, or houses, until the costs of the retrofits are recovered.

Today only twenty states permit decoupling of rates for electricity, natural gas, or both. Even in these states, some utilities don't do it, because even though conservation is a cheaper way to get power than building a new power plant, plant building is something they know how to do, and the ratepayers, not their shareholders, pay for it. Sometimes politicians won't do it for ideological reasons or because of pressure from interest groups that want to preserve the status quo. For example, Jim Rogers, the CEO of Duke Energy, America's third-largest coal consumer, wants to finance home and large building retrofits, but lacks the authority to do so. Of course, this means the ratepayers are being shafted and lots of jobs are being left on the table, but politicians get away with it because so few people understand the economics of energy.

So, if we're back to bank loans, the retrofits should start with the buildings sure to be in use with the same owners for five to seven years—public and private schools, federal, state, county, and local government buildings, college campuses, museums, libraries, auditoriums, hospitals, and big commercial buildings with limited indebtedness. If we just did the schools, colleges, and government buildings, we could keep a large number of construction workers busy for a couple of years.

When I first proposed this project in 2009, it met resistance in Washington from people who said it was unrealistic to quickly expand a retrofit market of $7 billion a year to $50 billion or more a year because a few big energy service companies, including Johnson Controls, Honeywell, and Siemens, have more than 90 percent of the business for big building retrofits. That's true, but not relevant to thousands of school buildings across the country that could also get an energy-savings guarantee from a local bonded general contractor who needs the business and doesn't want to lose skilled workers in a down economy.

The average school building is over forty years old and ripe for big savings, especially from more efficient heating and temperature controls. I'm sure you know of an old school building where on cool but not frigid days, the heat is on and the windows are open because the ventilation is poor and the temperature (and the energy use) can't be controlled.

Some school districts have been told that they can't borrow money to retrofit buildings because they're already at their debt limit, with property tax revenues pledged to pay off school-construction bonds. The rating agencies should exempt retrofits when calculating debt capacity because the schools don't take on new obligations; they just keep paying their utility bills at the same dollar amount until the costs are covered. If the savings don't cover the costs, the contractor makes up the difference. This is not like buying subprime mortgages.

The president's plan includes $25 billion for investments in school infrastructure. It's a good start, but the money could go even further if put into a loan guarantee fund and/or incentives to utilities to decouple and finance retrofits themselves.

10. **States and localities should have their own retrofit initiatives.** States can provide their own loan guarantees or mandate decoupling of rates. Beyond that, they can provide for payment of retrofit costs over time on property tax bills, on the theory that even if a building or a house changes owners, the utility bill still goes down, so the current beneficiary should pay the loan off. California has already passed legislation authorizing this procedure.

In some states, the electric co-ops are helping to finance retrofits. And whenever a city is served by a municipally owned utility, the public utility can decide to finance home and building retrofits with-

out seeking federal or state approval. It's interesting
that the only state in the country where all home-
owners are served by municipal utilities is conservative Republican Nebraska. Apparently, this is a
government function its citizens have decided not
to put on the antigovernment hit list. As a result,
Nebraska has provided fertile ground for a pioneer-
ing effort to offer homeowners an eight-hour retrofit, with utility savings averaging more than 20
percent.

Arkansas has a unique program called HEAL,
Home Energy Assistance Loan, in which employers first retrofit their buildings, then take the savings
and offer loans to their employees to retrofit their
homes. The employer is repaid from employees'
energy savings. The program was developed by my
foundation's Climate Initiative with a small grant
from the state's stimulus funding for clean energy.
Martha Jane Murray, the architect who runs the
program, also oversaw the Climate Initiative's work
on low-income housing retrofits in New Orleans
after Katrina, where 50 percent energy savings
were achieved. The idea behind HEAL is to make
workplace retrofits the norm and to create both the
demand and the financing for employee residential
upgrades. The work now under way with HEAL's
employers and their employees is already projected
to save $250,000 a year and to create a lot of jobs.
This is a public-private partnership that could be
set up anywhere. The savings achieved and the jobs

created should assure big-time expansion of the program.

The challenge with all these efforts is how to take them to scale. If Congress refuses to establish an infrastructure bank, states, big cities, or groups of states and cities could set up their own infrastructure bonds and perhaps attract some of the capital that would have gone to the national bank.

On retrofits, New York may have found the way to scale them. On August 4, 2011, Governor Andrew Cuomo signed a groundbreaking energy-efficiency financing program called on-bill recovery. Home-owners with modest incomes can all participate because they will repay the loans as a line item on their utility bill. The monthly loan repayment will be less than the savings they will realize from the benefits of the retrofit, thus providing a portion of the economic gain to the home-owner right away. It's estimated that over the next four years, one million homes and businesses could be retrofitted, creating ten thousand to twelve thousand jobs per year and saving New Yorkers an estimated $1 billion on their utility bills.

11. **Get the pension funds involved.** Public-employee and labor-union pension funds should finance investments in the infrastructure bank and in energy retrofits, especially for schools, colleges, and government buildings. They offer decent returns at very low risk and, unlike many investments in their portfolios, will create a lot of jobs,

many of them for union members. The AFL-CIO's president, Richard Trumka, and other union presidents, along with CalPERS, the California Public Employees' Retirement System, have already committed to raise $10 billion for this effort. This is a great opportunity for them and for the economy. At the Clinton Global Initiative in September 2011, Trumka and his partners announced that they had already secured more than a billion dollars for this effort.

12. **At least paint the roofs white.** The black tar roofs covering hundreds of thousands of American buildings, especially in older cities, absorb a huge amount of heat, requiring much more energy to cool the rooms below. Just painting the roof white can cut a building's energy use by up to 30 percent on a hot day. Every flat tar roof in every city and town should be painted white. Mayor Michael Bloomberg started a program in New York, the Green City Force, to train young people to do this work. A majority of them have been able to parlay their experience into high-skilled training programs or better-paying energy jobs. And lowering the electric bills 20 to 30 percent in every apartment or office frees up cash that utility customers can spend on other things.

We can get even greater energy savings and lower bills by planting greenery or growing gardens on rooftops. It costs more than painting because the roof has to be sealed to prevent leaking and strong enough to bear the extra weight, but the savings are greater. Chicago leads the nation in green roofs, but they're sprouting up everywhere.

Syracuse, New York, has started a program similar to Green City Force, Helping Hands, for unemployed people who didn't finish high school, training them to achieve even greater savings per building than Green City. Finally, thirty-five organizations and six federal agencies, funded by the Gates and Kellogg Foundations, are working together to create national opportunities for low-income young people in what they call the Green Career Pathways Framework. You can see that all this is good economics, for contractors, their employees, and people who pay utility bills. We just have to get the funding right. This is another example of how public, private, and not-for-profit cooperation works a lot better than ideological conflict.

Energy efficiency, if properly financed, can be an important job creator. And for those of us who agree with the 95 percent of climate scientists who say global warming is a big problem, efficiency is also a key element of the solution. The Center for American Progress estimates that the United States could achieve 50 percent of the reductions required to cut our greenhouse gas emissions 80 percent by 2050 through greater efficiencies alone.

13. **Reinstate the full tax credit for new green-technology jobs.** This tax credit has already helped

more than twenty-one hundred solar technology
start-up companies, as well as businesses making
other green-tech products. The only thing wrong
with it is that the total benefits were capped, resulting in a long waiting list of companies eager to create
new jobs that would boost the economy and make
us more energy independent. That is the kind of tax
break a job-starved economy needs, and it's about to
go away. Why?

In December 2010, with the Bush tax cuts about to
expire, the White House and Congress entered into
negotiations on which tax cuts to extend. Because
of the deficit, President Obama wanted to let the
rates on people earning $250,000 or more expire
while extending the Bush tax cuts for 99 percent of
Americans, along with other tax breaks, including
the green-tech projects. The Republicans said they
would block the extension of all the tax cuts, including those for the middle class, unless the green-tech
credit, called section 1603, was eliminated. At the
last minute, they finally agreed to extend it, but for
only one more year, so it's scheduled to expire at the
end of 2011.

Why did the antigovernment representatives
oppose section 1603? They said it wasn't a tax cut
at all; it was a spending program. You can decide
whether you agree. Here's how it works. A conventional tax credit doesn't help new companies,
because, in the early years of production, they don't
have income to offset the tax credit. Therefore, the

investment tax credit, for up to 30 percent of new capital expenditures, and the production tax credit of 2.2 cents per kilowatt hour of production don't help start-ups unless the credits can be sold to investors for money now. There hasn't been much of a market for buying tax credits since the recession began. To overcome this problem, section 1603 has allowed start-ups, mostly solar companies, to convert the credit into its cash equivalent since 2009. In the first two years of the program, $9.2 billion was distributed to support more than $31.1 billion in capital investment, including the over nineteen thousand solar projects and over four hundred wind projects. The 1603 credit is also projected to increase new wind energy installations 50 percent for every year it remains in place. Section 1603 plants are springing up all over the country. And as I said, there's a long waiting list of qualified companies that won't benefit from it and may not get off the ground unless the credit is extended beyond 2011. It's not such a high price to pay compared with China's incentives: free land, free worker training, and a twenty-year tax holiday.

Yet the antigovernment position is to let a proven job-creating tax break die while supporting the continuation of long-standing ones for companies already flush with cash, whether they are creating jobs in America or not. And calling 1603 a spending program, not a tax cut, is a weak attack. If section 1603 is a spending program, so are other business tax credits and deductions. That's why budget experts call them tax expenditures. If those tax breaks aren't spending, neither is section 1603. It's a cash advance on the investment tax credit so that it works for new companies as well as for established ones.

When I was in college, professors called this a distinction without a difference. When I was growing up in Arkansas, we called it straining at a gnat and swallowing a camel. That's what ideology and powerful vested interests will do to you. The provision has created a lot of good jobs in companies that will create a lot more. We need more jobs. It should be extended.

One of the reasons all Americans should support incentives like section 1603 is that over the next couple of years, several of our oldest, most polluting coal-fired power plants are scheduled to be shut down, and we need the capacity to replace them.

HERE ARE SOME RELATED job-creating ideas.

14. **Finish the smart grid, with adequate transmission lines,** at least enough to connect the areas where the wind blows hardest and the sun shines brightest to the population centers that use the most power. The stimulus legislation provided $17 billion for this purpose, a good start but not enough to cover all the areas of greatest opportunity for power generation and for job creation. Our grid is

divided into 140 largely autonomous areas of vary-
ing capacity. This leads to electricity disruptions
that cost the economy $100 billion a year. Fixing it
entirely would cost twice that but would provide a
quick return and allow 300,000 megawatts of wind
capacity and 4,000 megawatts of large solar projects
already planned to be built, because the electricity
they generate could be transmitted to users. If the
transmission capacity were there, North Dakota
alone could provide 25 percent of our nation's electricity demand with wind.

This is more important than ever, because the cost
of wind energy, if produced by turbines that qualify
for the production tax credit, is almost competitive
with fossil fuel generation now, and solar power, both
from photovoltaic cells and from large solar thermal
plants that capture the sun's energy to turn water
into steam that runs power generators, is expected
to reach parity over the next five years, because of
technological breakthroughs **and** the investment tax
credit. The price of both solar and wind drops mete-
orically as their volume increases, about 30 percent
each time capacity is doubled.

An additional benefit of connecting power generators in sunny, windy rural areas to urban grids is
that it will create good jobs in areas that have been
left behind for decades. For example, Americans
with the lowest per capita incomes are Native Americans who live on tribal lands too far from population centers to have profitable gambling operations.

With solar and wind power, virtually all of them could become energy independent, create new jobs, and generate substantial income that they could use to build more diverse, sustainable economies.

Besides ensuring the most efficient distribution of power across the nation as demand rises and falls in different places, a smart, connected power grid would enable utilities to reward customers willing to use power in off-peak hours, like washing and drying clothes late at night or early in the morning, when factories and office buildings are not up and running. Doing this nationwide would save all rate-payers money by reducing the need for extra power plants. An amazing amount of power plant capacity is idle most of the time. It's built to make sure we don't lose power on the hottest day of the year when everything that uses electricity is on. A smart grid and modern transmission lines could reduce the amount of excess capacity we need, saving money for businesses and consumers and creating jobs.

15. **Geothermal energy, using underground heat, should be increased.** Even with a superefficient system, we'll still need a lot of power to sustain growth, so we need to **maximize power generation from other domestic sources,** including geothermal, solid waste, and natural gas. The United States already leads the world in geothermal capacity, with 3,100 megawatts, though Iceland and the Philippines generate a higher percentage of their electricity with it

because of their unique geology. Because of stimulus funding, almost 8,000 megawatts of new geothermal capacity were added in 2010. With the tax incentives, the price of geothermal power, at three to five cents per kilowatt hour, is highly competitive. Because of the projects begun since 2009, employment related to the geothermal sector has more than doubled, exceeding fifty thousand jobs, with more on the way.

16. Not every community can develop geothermal power, but every community produces a lot of solid waste. **We should turn more landfills into power generators.** There are real benefits in converting solid waste into power: closing landfills; building recycling businesses in plastic, metal, glass, and organic fertilizer; and using the rest to provide steam heat to power factories or provide electricity for the grid. We could create jobs, improve public health, and free land for more productive purposes. Once the cost of a solid-waste plant is recovered, it's a great source of cheap power.

For an initial investment of $600 million in 1972, the city of Gothenburg, Sweden, built an efficient waste-to-energy generator that now saves its more than 500,000 citizens $33.6 million a year, reduces CO_2 emissions by 25 percent, and requires much less landfill space. São Paulo, Brazil, has power plants at the site of two of its large landfills. In India, New Delhi has just begun a large waste-to-energy project that my foundation's Climate Initiative helped to develop. In the 1980s, when I was governor of Arkansas, we had a steel wire plant that weathered the big downturn in manufacturing solely because its energy costs were lower than those of its competitors. The energy came from the local landfill. We should do a lot more of this.

17. **Develop our natural gas resources.** Many old coal-fired plants are scheduled to be closed in the next few years. They're big producers of carbon dioxide; the oldest 10 percent are responsible for about 40 percent of total CO_2 emissions from coal plants. As we develop other sources of clean power, we should use natural gas as a bridge fuel. It's the cleanest fossil fuel, more than 50 percent cleaner than coal in terms of greenhouse-gas emissions, 25 percent cleaner than oil when used in transportation, and only one-fourth as expensive. And new discoveries in the United States have given us a huge supply, enough for ninety years. I'd also like to see more natural-gas lines in the Northeast so that houses there could use it for heating. It's cheaper and cleaner than home heating oil.

The primary controversy over natural gas concerns the most efficient technology for its extraction, called fracking. It's alleged that the injections of a chemical solution into underground fissures to release and push the gas into more accessible and less costly recovery positions pollute water supplies and pose other health challenges. So far, studies in the areas where fracking has been most criticized don't seem to support the claim, but there is some troubling anecdotal evidence. State and federal officials with environmental protection responsibilities could allay public concerns by requiring extra care and monitoring of fracking, keeping it from being done too close to aquifers or other sources of drinking water. I also think the gas companies should disclose to the EPA the chemicals used in fracking so that any risks can be properly evaluated. Apparently many companies do so already, though they were exempted from having to in the 2005 energy bill, which I think was a serious mistake.

Natural gas also has great potential as a transportation fuel, as T. Boone Pickens has been arguing for years. My foundation has worked with cities in Latin America to install cleaner buses that run on concentrated natural gas, which can also power heavier trucks better than currently available electric battery technology. Transportation is responsible for about 25 percent of America's greenhouse-gas emissions, and oil imports comprise about half our trade deficit. The less we use gasoline to get around, the better off we'll be.

With proper care, I think we can extract the gas. We need it, and it can both make us more energy independent and contribute to job creation and growth.

18. **Keep developing more efficient biofuels.** In 2005, the United States adopted a requirement that renewable fuel usage be at least 7.5 billion gallons in 2012 and increase at a rate equal to the growth of gasoline after that. To achieve that goal, Congress passed a subsidy for the production of fuel from corn. In recent years, more than a third of our corn crop has gone to fuel production. The subsidy has been heavily criticized in the United States and abroad because of rising corn prices, global food shortages, and the relative inefficiency of corn ethanol compared with other biofuels. During the budget negotiations, there was bipartisan agreement to end the subsidy quickly.

That's good policy, though perhaps it would have been better to phase the subsidy out over three years. Regardless, it would be a mistake to abandon biofuels altogether. They help us to become more energy independent, and the fuel-processing plants create good jobs. The virtue of corn is that the cost of converting it into fuel is much less than that for other biofuel stocks, including switchgrass, rice hulls, and other biostocks widely available in the United States. The problem with corn is that it produces barely 2.5 gallons of biofuel for every gallon of oil required to make it, compared with 4 gallons or more for other biofuels and 9.3 gallons for fuel produced from sugarcane.

We should continue to promote biofuels, including biodiesel, by funding research to reduce conversion costs and providing tax incentives to help the ethanol plants switch to more efficient stocks when the corn subsidy dies. We should also consider changing the sugar subsidy to steer some of our own cane crop into biofuel. It might even help us with our obesity problem!

19. **Keep the tax credits for producing and buying electric and hybrid vehicles,** and increase the pace at which the federal automobile fleet is being converted. Our electric vehicle fleet is just getting off the ground, and it's already spurred new manufacturing companies whose founders believe they can compete with the all-electric Chevy Volt and Nissan Leaf, as well as the big-brand hybrids. My friend Terry McAuliffe went to China and bought one of their largest electric car companies and moved the entire operation to the United States, with two plants in Mississippi, and plans to expand to other states. We can't afford to lose this market to the Chinese, who are forging ahead, as are other nations, with electric-vehicle production.

Before we leave the transportation issue, I can't help noting the biggest step in the right direction the United States has taken lately. In late July 2011, President Obama announced an agreement involving Ford, GM, Chrysler, and ten other manufacturers accounting for 90 percent of U.S. auto sales, the United Auto Workers, environmental groups, state officials, and his administration to increase the average fuel economy of auto fleets to 54.5 miles per gallon by 2025. When fully in place, the new standards will cut carbon pollution in half and reduce fuel consumption 40 percent. The cleaner engines, more efficient transmission systems, lighter materials, and more aerodynamic designs required to meet the goal will create 150,000 American jobs, reduce our oil use by more than three million barrels a day, and save Americans $80 billion a year at the pump.

There was no fighting or name-calling, so it was a one-day story. Did you miss it? Don't miss the point. Conflict may work better in politics or in boosting the ratings of news programs, but **cooperation works better in real life**. Americans need victories in real life.

ONE THING THAT WOULD SPEED our much-needed transition to an energy strategy that produces more manufacturing jobs, lowers fuel bills, provides greater energy independence, and offers the possibility of averting the worst consequences of global warming is to have a large investor with enough market power to shape the future. The most obvious candidate is the U.S. military.

20. **The military can and should do more to speed our energy transformation.** Why? First, because the Pentagon, much to the chagrin of climate deniers in Congress, has recognized climate change as a threat to our national security. The Pentagon has con-

ducted war games and ordered intelligence studies to determine the range of problems that rising temperatures, droughts, food shortages, melting glaciers, and high sea levels present to our security, and it is working on a range of possible responses to them. Second, because the federal government is America's largest consumer of energy and the Department of Defense is responsible for 80 percent of it. And finally, because the military tries to make decisions based on evidence and has a proven capacity to solve problems in partnership with the private sector. The U.S. Army already has 126 renewable-energy projects under way.

I'm proud of the role that Hillary played in 2007, as a senator from New York and member of the Armed Services Committee, along with Senator John Warner, Republican of Virginia, a former secretary of the navy, in urging the Pentagon to assess the potential of climate change to threaten our security and to include its potential problems in making strategic plans. President Obama has supported this focus, and the Defense and State Departments have worked together to encourage Congress to adopt strong legislation to reduce the threats posed by global warming.

In a more immediate sense, the Pentagon also has a deep interest in proving that good energy policy can save money, because of the cuts in defense budgets the end of our involvements in Iraq and Afghanistan will bring and because more military-

budget cuts will be necessary to stem the government's long-term debt problem.

Secretary of the Army John McHugh, a former
Republican congressman from New York, and Secretary of the Navy Ray Mabus, a former Democratic
governor of Mississippi, have been especially active
in the search to save energy and get more of it from
renewable resources. McHugh has set up a task force
with a mandate to determine how the army can get
25 percent of its energy from renewable sources by
2025, with an investment of more than $7 billion in
a clean-energy infrastructure.

There are some real opportunities to save money
and enhance security. For example, shipping conventional fuel into high-temperature combat zones
just for air-conditioning costs the Pentagon billions
of dollars a year in fuel, transportation, security, and
medevac expenses. For Afghanistan, fuel is shipped
into Karachi, Pakistan, then driven eight hundred
miles on terrible roads for more than two weeks
through dangerous territory. A lot of U.S. soldiers
have been killed in those and other fuel convoys. If
our troops had had bases equipped with solar panels
to run the air conditioners and keep the lights on, it
could have saved money and lives and driven continued price reductions and technology improvements
beneficial to the entire economy. Solar cells, a few
backup generators with a small amount of fuel to
run them, and relatively inexpensive batteries that
store solar power for cloudy days could have made a

big difference in Afghanistan and Iraq and still can in many less hazardous places where our troops are deployed, including at forts in the United States. In the future, even if we rely more on our special operations forces like those who got Osama bin Laden, we'll still be called upon to help train security forces in other countries, we'll still have bases across the world, and we'll still need the military to develop and test new green technologies that will ultimately lead to similar money-saving, job-creating advances in the civilian economy.

THERE ARE AT LEAST THREE OTHER THINGS we could do in the energy area that would help the economy.

21. **Speed up the issuance of new energy efficiency rules for the most common household appliances.** President Obama asked the Energy Department to do this in February 2009. In the past, every time we have raised appliance standards, it's increased employment and cut utility bills. This round is estimated to save consumers $15 billion a year or more on their utility bills for the next three decades.

22. **Spend the rest of the rapid-rail money, but spend it where it will do the most good.** The Energy Department planned to finance thirteen

high-speed-rail corridors with $8 billion. After the
voters elected antigovernment governors in Florida, Ohio, and Wisconsin, those states returned the
funds. Now other states want the money. Conventional politics would argue for spreading the money
around, but I think it would be best to prove the
worth of high-speed rail with adequate investments
in heavily populated areas where there is a lot of
highway and airport congestion. Our fastest train,
Amtrak's Acela, which runs from Washington to
New York to Boston and back, travels about 100
mph slower than the fast trains that connect Japan's
most populous cities. If we build competitive, safe
networks in crowded areas, passengers tired of traffic delays, plane delays, and commutes to and from
airports in heavy traffic would flock to them. That
would build support for expanding high-speed rail
to other parts of the country and give us a chance to
work through any problems with the new systems.

23. **Support state and local innovations and
encourage their adoption across the country.** My
foundation is helping Los Angeles to install 140,000
superefficient LED streetlights that will save the city
$10 million a year in costs once the bulbs are paid
for. Los Angeles is also reducing pollution at its ports
with a "clean trucks" program that has increased sales
of more modern, efficient trucks, but the city has
been taken to court by the American Trucking Asso-
ciations, which is asserting the right of companies

to deliver cargo to the port in older, more polluting trucks. As noted earlier in this section, California passed legislation to allow building retrofits to be paid off through a line item on the owner's property tax bill for up to twenty years, but Fannie Mae and Freddie Mac are blocking federal legislation on the theory that the payment device is an encumbrance that would impact the value of mortgages it holds. If we put more people to work making houses more energy efficient, their value would increase, and so would the value of Fannie Mae's mortgage portfolio. Also, there really is no downside risk. Because the annual assessment on the property tax bill is set at a level equal to or less than the home-owner's savings on utility bills, it won't be harder to make the mortgage payments, so the risk of default won't rise.

The founding fathers saw states as laboratories of democracy. Today our cities are, too. Both states and cities are able to innovate in many areas that can ultimately benefit the entire nation. Energy efficiency is the perfect laboratory. It creates jobs, lowers costs, saves energy, and improves the environment. We should be clearing roadblocks to innovation, not erecting them.

24. **To speed up the process, we should pick one or two U.S. states or territories and work to make them completely energy independent.** The Energy Department could take competitive proposals and select one or two, three at most, for extra help in

maximizing their capacity to produce and consume energy. Nevada could do it, with its enormous solar and wind capacity. Making the effort would create jobs and lower its high unemployment and foreclosure rates. Puerto Rico could do it. Electric rates in the Caribbean are the highest in the world, because the base fuel is all imported. That hurts Puerto Rico's manufacturing sector and undercuts the value of the tax incentives Congress has provided to develop jobs there.

The one area where I disagree with the administration on energy policy is in the provision of large loan guarantees to nuclear power. Eighteen and a half billion dollars' worth of them have already been granted, and the administration has asked Congress for authority to issue $36 billion more.

I am not instinctively antinuclear. Arkansas has 2 of the 104 reactors that produce about 20 percent of America's electricity at sixty-five sites. I believe they're the two oldest continuously operating nuclear plants in the United States and they've worked well. I don't favor a rapid shutdown of the safely operating plants, as Germany and Japan have decided to do. But before we build more, we need to consider the relative economic and energy benefits of other options. We still haven't resolved the nuclear waste issues, and the Japanese tsunami and earthquake showed that power plants, like all other structures, are vulnerable to nature's forces. The industry is already heavily subsidized, yet new nuclear plants are basically uninsurable and so expensive to build that the estimated cost of power from them is twenty-five to thirty cents a kilowatt hour, three times today's rates and twice as high as solar power, which is dropping in price as new capacity comes on line and new technology improves productivity.

Finally, nuclear isn't much of a job creator compared with other clean fuel sources. A recent study by the Berkeley Renewable and Appropriate Energy Laboratory found that adopting a strategy that combines aggressive efficiency measures with generating 30 percent of our electricity from renewables would create **eight times as many jobs** as increasing our generating capacity the same amount by raising nuclear generation from 20 to 25 percent of our total, combined with capturing carbon from coal plants that provide 10 percent of our capacity. So I favor going for the options that offer the best combination of energy, environmental, and employment gains.

The economic benefits of clean-energy production and efficiency to ordinary Americans are enormous, both in new jobs and in lower costs. Of the thirty-seven wealthier nations obligated to reach specific reductions in greenhouse-gas emissions by 2012 under the Kyoto Protocol, four—Germany, the United Kingdom, Sweden, and Denmark—have made especially impressive efforts to reduce emissions. What happened? All of them have faster job growth, more rapidly rising incomes, lower unemployment, and less income inequality than the United States. The four countries adopted different economic and energy policies, implemented by both conservative and progressive governments. What they had in common was a serious commitment to change the way they produce and consume energy. Sweden got almost all of its reductions through greater efficiency, growing its economy more than 50 percent while reducing its carbon emissions 7 percent below 1990 levels. Germany did it by becoming the world's number-one user of solar cells, putting up a lot of windmills, and increasing efficiency. The U.K. did it by substituting natural gas for coal, developing its offshore wind capacity, and promoting large-scale efficiency projects.

Denmark is an especially interesting case. The Danes generate almost 25 percent of their electricity from wind, have biomass (waste-burning) power plants, and high home efficiency standards, including triple-paned windows, more insulation, heat pumps, and solar panels. Farmers are encouraged to put up their own windmills, which they can pay off in three years with savings from lower electricity costs, then earn a 12 percent profit on energy they sell to utilities. The results? The Danish economy expanded by 75 percent with no increase in fossil fuel use. We can do all of this and more.

THE PRODUCTION AND DEVELOPMENT of clean energy leads us naturally into the final opportunity for job creation in the president's strategy: doubling exports.

It's impossible to overstate the importance of doing this if we want to increase shared prosperity and reduce inequality. In early March 2011, two professors at New York University's Stern School of Business, the Nobel Prize winner Michael Spence and his colleague Sandile Hlatshwayo, released a fascinating study, **The Evolving Structure of the American Economy and the Employment Challenge.** They found that almost all our job growth over the last several years had come in "non-tradable" areas like government, health care, and other services like real estate and food services, while most of our income growth had come in "tradable" areas like high-end manufacturing, where productivity increased more in the jobs big companies kept in the United States, as they moved more of the less productive jobs offshore. Meanwhile, slower productivity growth in the non-tradable sector, and more competition for available jobs, kept wages and benefits from growing or even keeping up with inflation. The pattern has been reinforced by the recession. In 2010, low-wage jobs increased 3.2 percent, mid-wage jobs increased 1.2 percent, and high-wage jobs **decreased** 1.2 percent.

The only way to get out of this trap, according to Spence and Hlatshwayo, is to increase the size of the tradable sector of our economy. They don't argue for building trade barriers. We're only 4 percent of the world's population and still earn about a fifth of its annual income. We have to sell something to somebody else. There are more potential customers than ever. In 2009, the combined GDPs of Brazil, India, and China exceeded America's GDP for the first time.

More important for the subject of this book, Spence and Hlatshwayo also debunk the antigovernment myth that we can get out of this fix with lower taxes on the "job creators" and lower wages for workers. Instead, they say we need a national economic strategy. We have to change the incentives to make companies more willing to invest in making America more productive than in outsourcing more jobs.

To double exports, the U.S. strategy should include: building on our strengths, selling more of what we know people already want to buy; identifying products or services needed in growing markets that we can provide; making sure we have an intense, well-organized effort to promote what we're trying to sell to people who can buy it; providing adequate capital for U.S. exports and the overseas investments necessary to support them; getting small and medium-sized American businesses into export markets by helping them join together or partner with large U.S. companies to cut the costs and time delays of entering new markets; training men and women to do export-related work; and making sure we're playing by the same rules as our major competitors.

This is a pretty fair description of the Obama

administration's National Export Initiative. It has already expanded state export-promotion programs, given more resources and authority to the Export-Import Bank, and increased technical assistance and the availability of credit to small businesses that want to export.

To make this strategy work, we need to focus on three points. First, government policy matters a lot. All major exporting countries have aggressive public-private partnerships in which the governments promote the interests of their businesses and workers. If they do a better job than we do, they win. Second, the details matter a lot. The United States should concentrate on the markets, products, and services most likely to bring success. Third, whatever the rules are, they have to mean the same thing for all the major competitors. Reciprocity is important. The playing field is rarely perfectly level, so we have to be as willing as other countries to advance the interests of our own people.

Remember the story I told earlier about the federal government telling Los Angeles that in choosing between two foreign companies that wanted to supply the train cars for its rapid-rail network, the city couldn't give preference to the company that would make the cars in the United States over the one that would import them? That's because we're part of the World Trade Organization's Government Procurement Agreement, in which the signatories promise not to discriminate against each other's companies in bidding on government contracts. But what does that mean? Do we seriously think our competitors wouldn't find a way to distinguish between two U.S. companies competing to sell them the same products when one company was willing to create jobs in their nation and the other one wasn't?

HERE ARE A FEW SPECIFIC IDEAS that fit within the strategy.

25. **Concentrate on high-end manufacturing and getting smaller companies into exports.** This is what Germany does. It's one reason the Germans have penetrated China's growing market better than we have. The German unemployment rate is about 2 percent lower than ours, and Germany is the number-one exporter in the world. Exports account for more than 40 percent of its GDP, compared with 11 percent for the United States. We've got to do a better job. Taking a page from the German playbook, North Carolina has a good comprehensive program to get more small businesses into exporting, and Georgia has had some success in convincing American companies to move good manufacturing jobs back to the United States. We should replicate their successes all over the country.

26. **Negotiate long-term contracts to sell food to China, Saudi Arabia, and other nations facing food**

shortages. Feeding the world's growing population is a huge challenge and an opportunity. China's ability to feed itself has been reduced by expanding deserts and dropping water levels. More water and arable land are being lost every year to expanding cities, factories, and roads. The United States is the world's largest grain exporter, selling about ninety million tons a year. The end of the corn ethanol subsidy will free up more land to plant food for export, principally wheat and soybeans.

In the past few years, China, Saudi Arabia, and other countries with lots of money and limited capacity to feed themselves have bought or leased land in Africa and Asia to produce food, with minimal results for them and for the countries with the land. Foreign owners are far more likely than domestic ones to disrupt traditional farmers and to overutilize land and water, thinking they can always go somewhere else when the land plays out or there's no more water for irrigation.

A far better course is to build the capacity of developing countries to feed themselves, and increase the incomes of their farmers, with sustainable practices. Some of them will also become exporters but in a way that enhances their self-sufficiency and prosperity.

If we are willing to negotiate longer-term contracts to increase supplies of vital grains to China and Saudi Arabia at prices that would generate a good but not exorbitant income to our farmers, it would hold down big destabilizing spikes in food prices and buy the United States the time we need to reduce our reliance on China to buy our debt securities and on Saudi Arabia to keep imported oil flowing at affordable prices.

27. **Pass the pending trade agreements with South Korea, Colombia, and Panama.** We don't have a trade deficit in goods and services with the countries with which we have trade agreements. That's because the negotiations are tough and thorough, designed to meet both sides' needs, and supported by enforcement mechanisms. Our trade deficit is largely with the countries we buy oil from and the countries we borrow lots of money from, China and Japan.

28. **Enforce trade laws.** We lost manufacturing jobs in every one of the eight years after I left office. One of the reasons is that enforcement of our trade laws dropped sharply. Contrary to popular belief, the World Trade Organization and our trade agreements do not require unilateral disarmament. They're designed to increase the volume of two-way trade on terms that are mutually beneficial. My administration negotiated three hundred trade agreements, but we enforced them, too. Enforcement dropped so much in the last decade because we borrowed more and more money from the countries that had big trade surpluses with us, especially China and Japan,

to pay for government spending. Since they are now our bankers, it's hard to be tough on their unfair trading practices. This happened because we abandoned the path of balanced budgets ten years ago, choosing instead large tax cuts especially for higher-income people like me, along with two wars and the senior citizens' drug benefit. In the history of our republic, it's the first time we ever cut taxes while going to war.

29. **Concentrate on increasing the export potential of cities, not just states.** In 2010, the Brookings Institution issued a report, **Export Nation,** showing that our hundred largest metropolitan areas, already responsible for producing three-quarters of our GDP with two-thirds of our people, are best positioned to lead the drive to increase U.S. exports. In a nation where 13 percent of our GDP is in exports, even medium-sized cities, like Portland, Oregon, Youngstown, Ohio, and Wichita, Kansas, earn 15 percent or more of their income from trade. We need to get even more businesses in these areas involved in trade, by setting up centers that help smaller ones with the legal, financial, and other costs of entry, finding them trading partners in growing economies, and providing current and prospective employees with the necessary training, especially for jobs in manufacturing.

30. **Export more services.** We can export high-quality services not usually traded now, like edu-

cation, health-care, and consulting services. For example, we can use the Internet for things like tele-medicine, or send teams of people to other countries to develop services there, as U.S. universities have done recently in establishing universities in Qatar and the United Arab Emirates, or as Laureate International Universities has done, establishing a worldwide network of fifty-five universities in twenty-eight countries. We might be able to sell insurance policies in countries with a rapidly growing middle class, where life, property, and casualty policies are virtually nonexistent. People who know a lot more about this than I do should be charged with submitting a plan to maximize our exports in services.

31. **Get to emerging opportunities before others do.** The government can do more to help entrepreneurs and small-business people understand both what we can sell today and what we'll be able to sell soon.

Here's a great example. All over America, paper mills have closed, as we use less paper to communicate and other countries open their own mills. When a shuttered paper mill in southeast Virginia was put up for bid, Terry McAuliffe leased the forest and will install modern machinery that compresses wood waste into pellets with the same energy potential as lumps of coal. Two hundred fifty people will be hired to produce, pack, and ship the product. He'll be able to sell all he can produce to utilities in Europe that are required to reduce their carbon emissions and can't afford to close their coal plants. Instead, they'll burn 80 percent coal, 20 percent wood pellets. The market this year is eleven million tons, but in the next five years it will be ten times as large. And the utilities want a twenty-year supply. McAuliffe's plant is competitive because there is a lot of available wood waste, plus the availability of sustainably harvested timber; the plant is close to a port near the Atlantic Ocean, which keeps transportation costs down; and the production tax credit helps to finance the up-front costs of the machinery that makes the pellets.

There are closed paper plants all over the country that could produce pellets for export, especially those close to the Atlantic or inland river ports. This is also something that should have great marketability in China, where, in spite of poor air quality in much of the country and aggressive expansion of solar and wind generation, they're still building more coal-fired plants.

It's also an option for coal-fired plants in the United States. I think the coal companies should consider getting into this business themselves. The coal companies in the eastern part of the country operate in states that also have closed paper mills. They could offer both products to utilities and put people to work who've lost jobs in mills or mines. The EPA could help by offering utilities the opportunity to reduce CO_2 emissions to the required level by either closing plants, blending pellets with coal in more of them, or a combination of the two.

32. **Sell, sell, sell.** The president's National Export Initiative is, as I said, well conceived and comprehensive. But we still have to make the deals. Hillary is working hard to promote "commercial diplomacy" personally and to get our ambassadors and embassy staffs involved in increasing exports. It's vital to involve the Commerce Department and every other department and federal agency that can make a contribution to this effort, as well as governors, mayors, national business organizations, and American chambers of commerce in other countries. China's Export-Import Bank has a loan portfolio $20 billion larger than ours. That's more than 100,000 jobs' worth of difference. If we're going to shift our emphasis from more consumption to more production, we've got to be able to sell.

BEYOND THE IDEAS THAT FIT WITHIN the parameters of the president's job-generating priorities— building a twenty-first-century infrastructure, leading the world in green technologies, restoring our manufacturing base, and doubling exports— there are a few others I think we should consider.

33. **Increase the role of the Small Business Administration (SBA).** Our country's nearly thirty million

small businesses have created most of America's new jobs over the last fifteen years, generated more than half our nonfarm GDP, and paid the salaries of more than half our private-sector workers. If they were a single corporation, they would be "too big to fail." As it is, they're often too small for banks to lend to. In June 2011, Pepperdine University reported that more than half the small businesses surveyed said that their attempts to get more capital had been unsuccessful and that banks had denied 60 percent of small-business loan applications this year.

According to Gallup's chief economist, Dennis Jacobe, 40 percent of small businesses are hiring fewer people than they need. That's when the SBA is supposed to step in, offering loan guarantees of 50 to 85 percent for bank loans to small businesses, with 100 percent guarantees for disaster loans. Even when the SBA does offer guarantees, small businesses often find loans hard to come by. Despite benefiting from government bailouts and sitting on huge amounts of money, most banks have proved remarkably reluctant to make even guaranteed loans to small businesses.

A little history: The antigovernment Republicans have been hostile to the SBA since President Reagan tried to eliminate it and, failing that, to make sure it couldn't do its job. Their ideology holds that any small business worth its salt can get a bank loan without any help from the government.

As the Pepperdine and Gallup findings show, the

evidence doesn't support the ideology. SBA–backed investments have helped new businesses to grow into economic giants, including FedEx, Apple, Intel, Callaway Golf, Staples, Ben & Jerry's, Outback Steakhouse, Costco, Pandora, and Sun Microsystems.

President George H. W. Bush was a big supporter of small business and the SBA. He expanded its operations, including giving it the capacity to guarantee microloans to very small enterprises.

When I took office, I elevated the SBA to the cabinet and appointed two able administrators in Erskine Bowles and Aída Álvarez. During our eight years a simplified, expedited process doubled the overall number of SBA loans while more than tripling those to women and minorities.

President George W. Bush returned to the Reagan policy, cutting the budget by nearly 50 percent, cutting the staff by more than 25 percent, and freezing the microloan program.

President Obama is committed to reviving the SBA. He moved the budget back toward its all-time high in 2000 and added almost $1 billion more as part of his recovery initiatives, partly to fund two new programs: America's Recovery Capital (ARC) to provide up to $35,000 to help very small businesses get out of debt, and the Small Business Lending Fund (SBLF) to put money into struggling community banks so that they could lend to community businesses likely to be turned down by big banks. Neither program has been fully implemented, in part because of the erosion of the SBA's capacity to organize and administer such efforts over the last decade, in part because a lot of banks aren't interested in participating.

Getting loans to well-run businesses that want to increase hiring would make a significant contribution to our economy. I hope the president will put the SBA back in the cabinet, to make sure small businesses' concerns are fully aired in his ongoing effort to create jobs and to streamline government regulation (he's already proposed savings of $10 billion). To do its job well, the SBA must rebuild and modernize to make good decisions faster, starting with getting the ARC and the SBLF going full bore. If banks continue to resist making SBA–guaranteed loans, the SBA also should explore other ways to meet the demand. For example, it could broaden the definition of disaster loans to include the current economic emergency, so that loans of $100,000 or less could be made directly. Or it could increase the investment activity of the Small Business Investment Company, a public-private partnership administered by the SBA that puts long-term capital into private firms that invest in promising small and midsized businesses.

A lot of great companies started with SBA loans. It's time to get the loans going again.

34. Promote "crowdfunding" to help small businesses raise needed capital. "Crowdfunding" is the

term used for receiving small sums of money over the Internet. It allows start-ups or small businesses that are seeking to expand to raise money directly from individuals without going through a financial middleman. This has a real potential to fill the financing gap many small entrepreneurs face if they can't get conventional venture capital or a bank loan. Under current U.S. securities laws, which date back to the 1930s, money can only be raised from wealthy, knowledgeable investors, unless the businesspeople seeking capital go through a regulatory process that would cost more than the sum of money they're trying to raise.

President Obama has proposed an exemption from the securities laws for investments up to one million dollars. Representative Patrick McHenry, Republican of North Carolina, has a proposal to allow companies to raise up to five million dollars, with individual investments limited to ten thousand dollars or 10 percent of the investors' income, whichever is smaller. In 2010, the Sustainable Economies Law Center petitioned the SEC to allow investors to raise up to one hundred thousand dollars in contributions of no more than one hundred dollars per person. Even that would make a real difference. This is a reform that should get bipartisan support. In the U.K., just one business loan site is already raising more than two million dollars a month in crowdfunding.

35. Fill the three million jobs that are already open faster. Even though unemployment is high, posted job openings are being filled only half as fast as in previous postrecession economies. Part of the reason is that employers want particular skills applicants don't have. To speed up hiring, Michael Thurmond, former labor commissioner of Georgia, offered employers the money to train workers on-site. Employers don't pay payroll taxes or benefits during the training period, and they get the chance to fully evaluate people before they're hired. The Georgia Work$ system helps everyone. People get hired more quickly and spend less time on unemployment benefits. The federal government should ensure that every state offers this option. We can fill open jobs faster. President Obama embraced this idea in his American Jobs Act, and it should have bipartisan appeal.

36. **Provide an extra incentive to hire people who've been out of work more than six months.** More and more news reports indicate that employers, who can be very choosy in hiring in this environment, are reluctant to hire, sometimes even to interview, people who've been out of work more than six months. I think that's understandable but still a mistake. Many of the longer-term unemployed are hardworking, reliable people who spent months trying to find jobs they know how to do or jobs paying close to what they used to make. To encourage employers to give them a chance, we should give them, in addition to whatever is available for all new hires, a longer payroll-tax holiday,

one month for every month beyond six months a new hire was unemployed. President Obama's plan has a different and probably better idea: $8 billion to fund a tax credit to businesses that hire the long-term unemployed.

37. **Give employers an incentive not to lay off workers in the first place.** One reason the German unemployment rate is 2 percent lower than ours is that in tough times, employers and employees can agree to reduce everyone's hours and pay in a system called Kurzarbeit, "short work." The government encourages this instead of layoffs by paying the employee 60 percent of his or her lost wages. It's cheaper than full unemployment payments, keeps skilled workforces intact, and helps the economy recover. We should adopt a version of it. Earlier in this book, I told the story of Nucor steel and the benefits of its no-layoff policy. The president's plan provides $49 billion in expanded unemployment benefits, with the provision that some of it can be used to test the idea in areas where it's most likely to work. I'm convinced this kind of system would increase our long-term productivity and keep unemployment lower. We should have instituted it years ago.

38. **"Insource" jobs we've been outsourcing.** At the Clinton Global Initiative America meeting on the U.S. economy, in June 2011, one of the most impressive commitments to create jobs was made by

Onshore Technology Services. Onshore was founded in 2006 to retrain underemployed and dislocated workers in information technology. The company offers business customers the chance to **reduce their IT costs 25 to 35 percent without sending the work offshore.** Onshore has committed to develop an operations center with a thousand employees in Joplin, Missouri, to help it recover from the tornado damage, and to create twelve thousand jobs throughout rural America. We need more of these efforts and should encourage them with support from the Department of Commerce, which could identify potential corporate customers for insourcing, and from the SBA, which could help with initial capital.

39. **To support the insourcing movement,** we should **increase the number of empowerment zones and expand the reach of the New Markets Initiative.** These two initiatives, which began during my administration, give businesses extra incentives to invest in areas of very high unemployment or low per capita incomes. Expanding them would have to include incentives over and above the broad-based ones of the American Jobs Act. For example, we could provide free training and the cash equivalent of a ten-year property-tax holiday for investments that create more than a certain number of jobs or reopen a closed factory.* Those are investments that

*This is an idea I first heard suggested by Newt Gingrich.

wouldn't be made otherwise, and the new employers and their employees would pay income taxes. More important, they'll have jobs.

40. Increase the preparation and recruitment of, and incentives for, more young Americans to get degrees and take jobs in STEM (science, technology, engineering, and mathematics) fields. For example, we should forgive student loans in return for a certain number of years' work in these areas. Decades ago, we did the same thing to lure young doctors to medically underserved parts of the country, and it worked.

41. Keep pushing for comprehensive immigration reform, and in the meantime grant more H-1B visas to immigrants in STEM fields until we have enough qualified citizens to fill the openings. President Obama has improved border enforcement and increased deportation of illegal immigrants. It's time to give those who are working, raising kids, and paying taxes a path to citizenship. If Congress can't agree to that, at least immigrants who have jobs and pay taxes should be able to get work permits while we work on the larger problems a proposal President Reagan supported in the 1980s. We should also encourage gifted young immigrants who've grown up here to get a college education and become productive citizens. Pulling students out of college and sending them home, or making it too expensive to go by denying them in-state tuition at colleges in that state where they grew up and their parents pay taxes is not going to help our economy. Remember, it's an advantage for the United States to have a workforce younger than those of Japan and Europe.

Meanwhile, the immigrants who fill the STEM jobs will help to increase employment for citizens, increase exports, and bring back manufacturing, so we should issue as many H-1B visas as necessary to fill the STEM jobs that can't be filled by Americans.

42. **Bring more tourists to the United States.** Spending on global travel is already at $1 trillion and is projected to double by 2020, with almost three hundred million people a year traveling outside their own countries. An increased effort in this area should have strong support. According to a study by the U.S. Travel Association, overseas visitors spend an average of $4,000 on U.S. services and products, and one new job is created for every thirty-five new visitors. Unlike most countries that derive a lot of income from tourism, the United States didn't have a national effort to market itself abroad until early 2010, when Congress passed, with a large bipartisan majority, and the president signed the Travel Promotion Act. The act created the Corporation for Travel Promotion (CTP), a public-private partnership overseen by a board of directors appointed by the secretary of commerce and funded, not by U.S. taxpayers, but from $10 of the fees paid by visitors

from visa waiver countries and private-sector contributions on a fifty-fifty basis.

Because of the widespread belief that it is more difficult to come to the United States after 9/11 and other negative stereotypes, we need to accurately brand the United States as a desirable travel destination and reach out to the millions of people who still feel a strong kinship to our country. The CTP's first marketing efforts will begin later this year at an international travel event in London.

It's important that the entire government, from the White House on down, support this effort. The State Department is already putting staff resources into it as part of its commercial-diplomacy push. And it's critical that the travel industry in every state participate aggressively in trade shows, social media outreach, and through the website, through other marketing efforts, and with the production of unique multistate travel packages.

International travel already supports nearly two million jobs in America, according to CTP. If we do this well, the initiative could create hundreds of thousands more.

43. **Promote affordable opportunities to "buy American."** Roger Simmermaker, an electronics technician from Orlando, Florida, is the author of **How Americans Can Buy American.** It contains more than sixteen thousand products and services made in the United States and includes a special list

of a thousand union-made products. Simmermaker also offers Americans a free e-guide to more than twenty-five hundred products available in popular retail outlets like Dillard's, Home Depot, and Costco.

Diane Sawyer, the anchor of ABC's **World News,** has asked Americans to join her in pledging to buy more goods made in America, saying that if all Americans on just one occasion spent just $3.33 more on goods made here, it would create ten thousand jobs. I'm not trying to put the importers and all the people who work for them out of business. I have shoes and clothes that are both made in America and imported. But today only 25 percent of our money spent on shoes and clothes goes for U.S.–made products. If we just raised it to 30 or 35 percent, we could create a lot of jobs in manufacturing and throughout the supply chain. To help us make an American choice, on these and other issues, a Florida company, Made in USA Certified, verifies companies' claims that their materials and manufacturing are domestic.

44. **Support National Jobs Day.** On November 1, 2011, a group of business leaders urged the more than one million companies with fifty or more employees to hire just one unemployed person. The idea was the brainchild of Jerry Jones, chief legal officer of Acxiom. The objective is to get at least a million people hired by Thanksgiving. Jones argues

that it is in the business community's interest to create more consumers, that companies with more than
fifty employees can afford to do it, and that putting
a million people to work might change the prevail-
ing negative psychology enough to spark even more
hiring. This is one of those ideas that sounds too
good to be true but may just be true.

45. **Offer an X Prize or its equivalent for ideas
that promote innovation and job creation.** Every
day, the press and blog sites carry new ideas their
proponents claim will create lots of jobs. In an article in the **Wall Street Journal,** Andy Kessler argued
that freeing up the unused and underutilized spectrum, including that which is government owned,
could "create a million new jobs, not to mention
new devices and apps not thought possible in our
bandwidth-starved world—phones that work in ele-
vators and subways, remote auto and medical diag-
nostics, real-time ads on smart phones and other
devices . . . and that's just in the first six months." I
don't know if he's right, but it's worth testing.

The X PRIZE Foundation runs large-scale com-
petitions with generous prizes for ideas that lead
to products worth more than the prize itself. For
example, it's offered prizes for the development of
a car that gets a hundred miles per gallon and for
commercially viable space travel. It's independent
of both the government and private interest groups,
and wealthy individuals could be recruited to fund

the prizes. I'd like to see them awarded on a sliding scale based on the number of jobs created, with a ten-thousand-job minimum. If the X PRIZE Foundation won't do it, someone will. This would be a great commitment for the Clinton Global Initiative.

46. **Replicate the prosperity centers.** Earlier in the book I described the prosperity center built around computer simulation in the Orlando area. The cooperative synergies of Disney's and Universal's theme parks, Electronic Arts' video games division, Defense Department and NASA training programs, and the University of Central Florida's education, training, research, and technology-transfer capacity have attracted more than one hundred other companies involved in simulation work, from corporate giants like Lockheed Martin to small start-ups with big dreams.

I first read about Orlando's unique cluster in **The Next American Economy** by William J. Holstein. The book tells a lot of other success stories. MIT's well-run technology-transfer program, plus a $100,000 Small Business Innovation grant from the SBA, helped start a remarkable new battery company called A123 Systems, which now has more than sixteen hundred employees in the United States and Asia and is building a new battery factory in Michigan to employ hundreds more.

In 1980, Congress authorized universities to transfer technology developed with federal research money to the private sector. Virtually all of them look for opportunities to do so and to make money doing it. A young relative of mine does this work for Texas A&M and is involved in some exciting projects. But MIT's system is arguably the best in the country. They don't charge new companies anything up front. Instead, they take stock in the new companies and hope for big returns if their technology proves profitable. It's a model other universities should be encouraged to adopt.

In Pittsburgh, Carnegie Mellon University is helping the city of steel become the city of advanced robotics, with more than thirty new companies already up and running, many with support from the Defense Department, NASA, and private companies like Boeing.

San Diego now has more winners of Nobel Prizes in the sciences than any other American city as the capital of America's genomics industry, beginning with the work of the biotech legend Craig Venter and the commitment of the University of California at San Diego to build a world-class supercomputing center. Thanks to the wireless communications pioneer Irwin Jacobs's company, Qualcomm, San Diego is also home to seven hundred or so wireless communications firms and is now building one of the top wireless health centers in the United States.

There are lots of other stories in Holstein's book that will encourage you to believe in America's capacity to create good jobs: how Corning innovated internally to develop Gorilla Glass to replace the easy-to-shatter plastic on cell phones; how Austin, Texas, is mobilizing to create a smart power grid with more solar and wind power in the hands of individual citizens and businesses who can sell what they don't use back to the grid; how North Carolina is organizing to increase the number of small- and medium-sized businesses that export; how Cleveland's Cuyahoga Community College has been especially successful in retraining older unemployed workers for good jobs that are available; how Georgia is bringing lost manufacturing jobs back to the United States; and, of course, how Silicon Valley is booming again.

In July 2011, Mayor Bloomberg announced a plan to make New York City "the technology capital of the United States, and the world," offering land and $100 million in infrastructure upgrades to any university, educational institution, or consortium to build a science and engineering campus on Governors Island, Roosevelt Island, or the Brooklyn Navy Yard. There are already a lot of universities in the city. I hope they'll offer a joint proposal, plus a plan to transfer their discoveries to start-ups in return for an ownership share, as MIT does. There also needs to be a fund to provide seed capital to start-ups. New York could then rival Silicon Valley and tech communities all over the world as a prosperity cluster.

The Startup Foundation is hosting summits all over America to identify the opportunities in and obstacles to establishing entrepreneurial ecosystems. In New York State, Governor Andrew Cuomo has organized a competition for development funds among ten regional economic clusters. It is modeled on the Federal Empowerment Zone program and requires leaders within each region to work together to develop ambitious but achievable development plans.

The federal government should increase support for these and other new innovation centers and encourage all states and large metropolitan areas to develop them.

In an August 31, 2011, article in **USA Today,** Michigan's former governor Jennifer Granholm and Daniel Mulhern suggested, as I have, repatriating offshore earnings of American corporations at the 15 percent capital gains rate and using a lot of the money to fund a "Jobs Race to the Top," modeled on the Department of Education's Race to the Top program, in which effective public-private partnerships would compete for grants and no-interest loans. It's a good idea.

These kinds of innovation clusters can spring up everywhere in America. They're models of freedom, creativity, and **cooperation.** Innovators, entrepreneurs, patient investors, venture capitalists, established companies, private foundations, universities, community colleges, and federal and state agencies work together in ways that create jobs, good incomes, and wealth.

In other words, made-in-America prosperity looks nothing like the food fight in Washington. Its hallmark is cooperation, not conflict. The private sector views its public sector partners as indispensable allies, not the tax-grabbing, wealth-robbing predators of antigovernment mythology. When you're actually trying to create new businesses, new jobs, and new wealth, you do what works.

We all need to do what works. And we don't have a day or a dollar to waste.

EPILOGUE

Time to Choose

WHAT KIND OF FUTURE DO WE want? Do we want a country where we work together to restore the American Dream and rebuild the middle class? What's the smart, effective way to do that? With a strong economy and a strong government working together to advance shared opportunity, shared responsibility, and shared prosperity? Or with a weak government and powerful interest groups who scorn shared prosperity in favor of winner take all until it's all gone? That's really where antigovernment, "you're on your own" policies will lead us.

If we want a future of shared prosperity, where the middle class is growing and poverty is declining, where the American Dream is alive and well, and where the United States remains the leading force for peace and prosperity in a highly competitive world, we've got a lot to do, and we need to get moving.

Everywhere we look, across the world and within the United States, prosperity is produced by networks of people committed to productive investment over unaffordable consumption, to creative cooperation over constant conflict.

It won't be easy to create a prosperity environment everywhere in America, not only because conditions and resources vary so much, but also because thirty years of bipolar antigovernment politics have given us a severe case of collective attention deficit disorder. We respond predictably to the same old adrenaline shots from politicians and pundits. We don't much like being around, listening to, or learning from people who disagree with us. And we worry that our best days may be behind us.

They may be. But they don't have to be.

When a lifelong Democrat, Bill Bishop, can write in his book, **The Big Sort,** that he misses his talks and arguments with his only Republican neighbor, who moved across town in Austin to a heavily Republican area because, except for Bishop, his Democratic neighbors made him feel uncomfortable, there's hope.

When a lifelong Republican, John Bogle, who pioneered the indexed mutual fund, can write in his book **Enough** that the financial sector has taken too much out of the American economy by focusing on high-dollar transactions that have large fees but make no contribution to the growth of companies or employment, then join other successful Republicans and Democrats in proposing drastic changes to reduce the obsession of Wall Street and corporate America with "short-termism," there's hope.*

As long as Americans by the thousands keep lining up for every open job, and young (and not so young) people keep coming up with good ideas, there's hope.

To turn that hope into positive changes, Americans in all walks of life have to muster the confidence, common sense, and creative imagination to get our country out of its economic and political rut and back onto the road to the future.

In a Gallup poll in the spring of 2011, fewer than half of Americans surveyed believed the current generation of young adults will have a better life than their parents. An August 14, 2011, article in the **Los Angeles Times** titled "Generation Vexed: Young Americans Rein in Their Dreams" documented how young people are altering their career plans, putting off marriage, and downsizing their dreams.

I can understand the pessimism of the young. After all, we've been mired in the current mess for a significant portion of their lives. But giving up is not a strategy for success. Downsizing budgets may be necessary, but downsizing dreams is a decision to be disappointed.

*A report by the Aspen Institute, **Overcoming Short-termism: A Call for a More Responsible Approach to Investment and Business Management,** is really worth reading, for the sweep and the specificity of its bipartisan proposals to reform the financial sector to create more jobs and long-term value, including a tax on financial transactions that has bipartisan business support. See http://www .aspeninstitute.org/sites/default/files/content/images/Overcoming% 20Short-termism%20AspenCVSG%2015dec09.pdf.

There is one thing we can't change. We are rapidly becoming more and more enmeshed in an interdependent world, one with more rising economic powers and more widely dispersed political influence. Anybody who was thinking about it on the day the Berlin Wall fell realized then that America had become the world's sole economic, political, and military superpower but that it couldn't last very long. If you believe that intelligence and effort are equally distributed, then you shouldn't begrudge the fact that our interdependent world is bound to give more people in other nations the chance to claim their dreams, more nations a chance to rise or to reinvent themselves and rise again. And if you really believe in freedom and free markets, you shouldn't complain about the competition but learn from it.

In this new, multipolar world, we can still be the world's best innovator; the world's best producer of new products and services; the world's best assimilator of people from every nation, race, religion, and culture; and the world's best example of shared opportunity and responsibility, demonstrating the power of both individual freedom and close cooperation and proving both the genius of free markets and the necessity of active government.

Success in the twenty-first-century world requires Americans to be curious enough to learn from countries that are doing important things better than we are, humble enough to listen and to learn from Americans who disagree with us, smart enough to realize that shared prosperity is a better formula for success and happiness than "you're on your own," and big enough to admit we're all going to be wrong once in a while. (If you want to feel better about not being perfect and see the potential upside in your errors, read **Being Wrong** by Kathryn Schulz.)

We're in a mess now. At the dawn of the new century, after years of strong job growth, rising incomes, and declining debt, we abandoned a proven path to shared prosperity in favor of doubling down, once more, on antigovernment ideology. Now we're paying for it. The only sensible thing to do is for all of us to take some responsibility for changing things. The world is moving on, and if we want to stop falling behind, we have to get back in the game. Let's ditch the stale certainty of ideology and bring our values, ideas, experiences, and dreams to a real debate about the future. Think how exciting it would be if all of us—Democrats, Republicans, and independents, conservatives, liberals, progressives, and libertarians—had real arguments based on real facts that produced real results through principled compromise based on what works.

I don't know how this will turn out. I just know that for more than two hundred years, everyone who's bet against the United States has lost. A lot of people are betting against us today. I'm betting that once again, in a very different world, we'll find our way to a "more perfect Union." Let's get the show on the road.

ACKNOWLEDGMENTS

As in the writing of **My Life** and **Giving,** I am most indebted to Justin Cooper for helping me gather and organize materials, doing extra research, fact-checking, and correcting errors, and working with me to make the book clearer as I wrote and rewrote it. Justin was assisted with fact-checking in the final weeks by Betsy McManus and Caitlin Klevorick.

My editor, Bob Gottlieb, and managing editor, Katherine Hourigan, were, as always, invaluable in making sure that in substance and style the book would be interesting and useful to all kinds of readers.

I am also grateful to others at Knopf for their support. Sonny Mehta, chairman and editor in chief; Tony Chirico, president; Carol Carson, Maria Massey, Jessica Freeman-Slade, Andy Hughes, Virginia Tan, and the many others who did the proofreading and put the book together in record time.

I want to thank all those who read all or part of the book and offered suggestions, beginning with Hillary, Chelsea, my lawyer Bob Barnett, Doug Band, Oscar Flores, Rolando Gonzalez-Bunster,

Bruce Lindsey, Terry McAuliffe, John Podesta, Matt McKenna, and Mark Weiner.

I am indebted to the many people who provided information and insight on the mortgage crisis, the corporate tax reform system, and other issues and ideas discussed in the book.

While I was writing this book, the work of my foundation, presidential library and center, the school of public service, the Clinton Global Initiative, and our work in Haiti continued, thanks to the efforts of the many good people who work in those areas. I am profoundly grateful to all of them. I want to especially thank Laura Graham, my chief of staff and representative in all our Haiti efforts; Ginny Erlich, who leads the Alliance for a Healthier Generation; Bob Harrison and the staff of CGI; Ira Magaziner and the staff of CHAI; Ami Desai, my foreign-policy aide and liaison to the Clinton Climate Initiative.

Finally, I want to thank those who make the work I do today possible with their donations of time and money. They span the political spectrum, all income and age groups, and live all over America and across the world. Every day, they prove cooperation works better than conflict.

PERMISSIONS ACKNOWLEDGMENTS

Grateful acknowledgment is made to the following for permission to reprint previously published material.

The charts on pages 45, 46, 47, 122, and 132 are © 2011 **New York Times.** All rights reserved. Used by permission and protected by the Copyright Laws of the United States. The printing, copying, redistribution, or retransmission of this Content without express written permission is prohibited.

    p. 45: Excerpted from **New York Times/ Boston Globe** graphic "The Debt Crisis," July 31, 2011.

    p. 46 and p. 47: July 24, 2011.

    p. 122: February 19, 2011.

    p. 132: August 5, 2011.

The charts on pages 127 and 138 are from the OECD (Organisation for Economic Co-operation and Development).

    p. 127: OECD (2010), Education at a

Glance 2011: OECD Indicators, OECD Publishing, http://dx.doi.org/10.1787/8889 32459831.

p. 138: OECD Tax Revenue Statistics, OECD Tax Database, www.oecd.org/ctp/taxdatabase, accessed on 9/26/2011.

LIKE WHAT YOU'VE READ?

If you enjoyed this large print edition of
BACK TO WORK,
here is another one of Bill Clinton's latest
bestsellers also available in large print.

GIVING
(paperback image)
978-0-7393-6808-4
($24.95/$29.95C)

Large print books are available wherever books
are sold and at many local libraries.

All prices are subject to change. Check with your
local retailer for current pricing and availability.
For more information on these and other large print titles,
visit www.randomhouse.com/largeprint.